PERCUSSION EDITI

BOOK TWO

Band Expressions

Band Expressions Author Team
Co-Lead Author: **Robert W. Smith**
Co-Lead Author: **Susan L. Smith**
Michael Story **Garland E. Markham** **Richard C. Crain**
Contributor: **Linda J. Gammon**
Percussion Contributor: **James Campbell**
Editor: **Thom Proctor**
Assistant Editor: **Patrick Roszell**
Assistant Editor: **Heather Mahone**

Art Credits:

Page 14: *Sunday, Music in the Country* by Raoul Dufy (1877–1953), © 2006 Artists Rights Society (ARS), New York/ADAGP, Paris. 1942-43. Musee d'Art Moderne de la Ville de Paris, Paris, France. Photo credit: Bridgeman-Giraudon/Art Resource, NY.

Page 14: Photo of Henry Fillmore courtesy of the University of Miami, Frost School of Music.

Page 20: *The Great Wave of Kanagawa from the series "36 Views of Fuji"* by Katsushika Hokusai (1760–1849), Color woodblock print.10 1/8 x 14 15/16 in. (25.7 x 37.9 cm). 1831–1833. Private collection. Photo credit: Art Resource, NY

Page 24: Photo of Clare Grundman courtesy of Boosey & Hawkes, Inc.

Page 24: *Nine Lives* from "In a Nutshell: Charlie the Red Cat" by Jim Tweedy, © 1993 by Jim Tweedy.

Page 32: Photo of African village and drums Bangui: Central African Republic. © SuperStock, Inc.

Page 34: *Two Over Three* by Tom Berg. Oil on canvas. 30 x 40 in. © 2001 Tom Berg.

Page 34: Photo of Ralph Vaughan Williams © Bettmann/CORBIS.

Page 38: Illustration of Scott Joplin by Magdi Rodriguez, © 2005 Alfred Music Publishing, Inc.

Page 38: *Vampin' (Piney Brown Blues)* by Romare Bearden (1914–1988). © Romare Bearden Foundation/Licensed by VAGA, New York, NY. Photo Credit: Smithsonian American Art Museum, Washington, D.C./Art Resource, NY.

Book 2

* Please refer to the Art of Playing in Book One for more information.

The Art of Playing Percussion

Dynamics

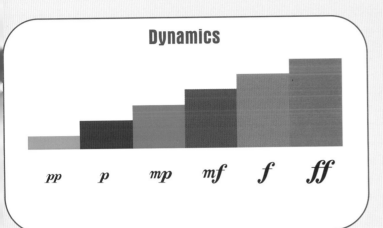

pp   p   mp   mf   f   ff

Dynamic Markings

pp — the symbol for pianissimo, meaning to play very soft

p — the symbol for piano, meaning to play soft

mp — the symbol for mezzopiano, meaning to play medium soft

mf — the symbol for mezzoforte, meaning to play medium loud

f — the symbol for forte, meaning to play loud

ff — the symbol for fortissimo, meaning to play very loud

Articulation

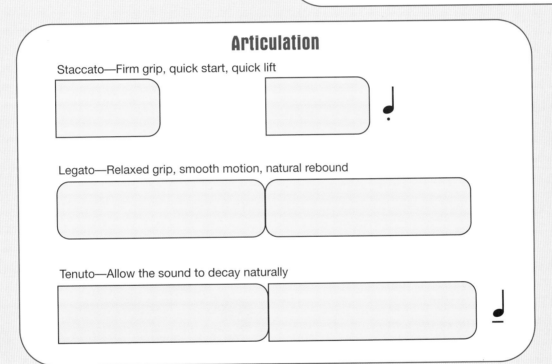

Staccato—Firm grip, quick start, quick lift

Legato—Relaxed grip, smooth motion, natural rebound

Tenuto—Allow the sound to decay naturally

Rhythm Chart

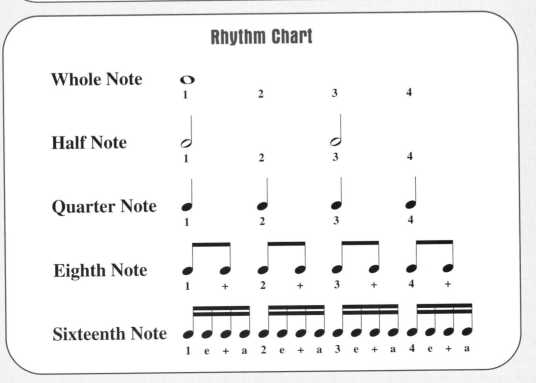

Whole Note	1	2	3	4
Half Note	1	2	3	4
Quarter Note	1	2	3	4
Eighth Note	1 +	2 +	3 +	4 +
Sixteenth Note	1 e + a	2 e + a	3 e + a	4 e + a

The Art of Playing Snare Drum

Instrument and Parts

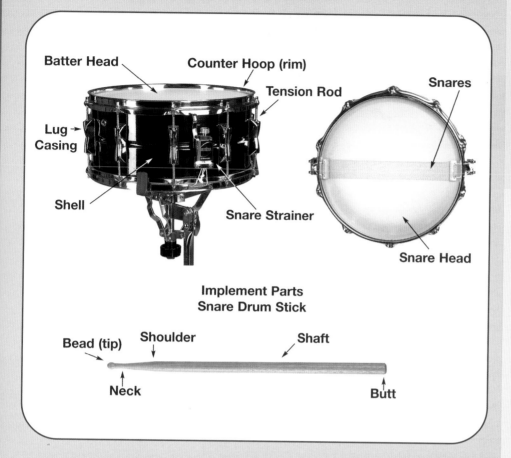

Batter Head
Counter Hoop (rim)
Tension Rod
Snares
Lug Casing
Shell
Snare Strainer
Snare Head

Implement Parts
Snare Drum Stick

Bead (tip)
Shoulder
Shaft
Neck
Butt

History

1. The snare drum can be traced back more than 250 years to large drums used by military bands as signals to the troops, as well as for ceremonial functions.

2. During the latter part of the nineteenth century, the snare drum was found in use by opera orchestras and gradually appeared more regularly in symphonic works.

Advanced Care and Maintenance

- Use a cloth to keep the entire drum clean and free of fingerprints, dust, and dirt.

- Keep all objects off of the drum head; it's not a table.

- The average life of a drum head is often less than one year. Replace worn or damaged heads immediately.

- A small dab of lithium grease or lubrication should be applied to the tension rods when the heads are replaced.

Setup Procedure

1. The snare drum should be flat and parallel to the floor with the snare strainer placed directly in front of you.

2. Adjust the stand to bring the top head to approximately waist level or slightly below.

3. It may be helpful to mark the stand height with a felt marker to ensure a consistent setup every time the instrument is assembled. This can be checked from time to time as you grow.

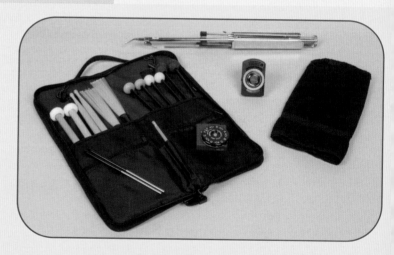

Storage Procedure

1. Store the drum and stand in its case with the snares engaged when not in use.

2. Cases are for your instrument only, not for sticks, music, folders, or books.

3. Store the sticks in a stick bag with all of your mallets and accessories.

Supplies

- Snare Drum Sticks, concert model, pair
- General timpani mallets, pair
- Plastic bell mallets, pair
- Triangle beaters, pair
- Yarn mallets, pair
- Hard rubber mallets, pair
- Brushes, pair
- Pitch pipe (timpani tuning
- Stick towel (black hand towel)
- Stick/Mallet Bag
- Drum key
- Metronome
- Pencil
- Wire Music Stand

Please refer to the Art of Playing in Book One for more information.

The Art of Playing Bass Drum

Instrument and Parts

Edge
Off-Center
Center

History

1. The bass drum was introduced to the Western orchestra through Turkish military bands of the seventeenth and eighteenth centuries.

2. The large, double-headed concert drum is considered the "heartbeat" of the concert band.

3. It is most resonant when the instrument is mounted on a suspension stand; it creates a low, indefinite pitch.

Setup Procedure

1. The drum should be tilted to reflect sound toward the conductor and the audience.

2. Set the music stand so that you can see the bass drum head, the music, and the conductor.

3. Match the size of your bass drum beater to the size of your drum. A good, general beater has a soft felt covering over a hard core.

Playing Areas

1. Off center: Strike the head here to produce the low resonant tone used for most playing situations.

2. At center: Strike the head here for the driest sound, when clarity is needed for quick repeated passages, or to create a cannon-shot effect.

3. Edge: Play with two mallets near the edge when producing rolls.

Tuning

- The playing side is tuned low to achieve a deep, resonant tone. Tune the resonating head slightly higher than the playing side.

Rolls Play Position

- A matched pair of beaters is used for rolling on the bass drum that is smaller and lighter than the standard beater.

- Set the bass drum in a horizontal position and grip the beaters the same as for timpani mallets for rolls.

- Use quick, single alternating strokes to sustain the roll. Always allow the beaters to naturally rebound off the head.

- Softer volumes are produced near the edge while louder rolls are performed closer to the center of the head.

Advanced Care and Maintenance

- Use a cloth to keep the entire drum clean and free of fingerprints, dust, and dirt.

- Keep all objects off of the drum head, as it's not a table.

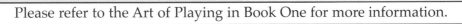

Please refer to the Art of Playing in Book One for more information.

The Art of Playing Timpani

Instrument and Parts

Counter Hoop (rim)
Head
Tuning bolt
Tuning Gauge
Strut
Bowl
Caster (with wheel lock)
Pedal

History

1. Timpani (kettledrums) found their way to Europe in the fifteenth century as military instruments mounted in pairs on horseback.

2. In the seventeenth century, timpani starting being performed in the orchestra in support of the trumpet part with much of their music being improvised by highly skilled performers.

Timpani Ranges

- Set each timpano into proper range by tuning the head to its fundamental note when the pedal is at its lowest position.

- 32" – D, 29" – F, 26" – B♭, 23" - d

Setup Procedure

1. The pedals should face the player and pointed pointed slightly inward toward the player.

2. Stand behind the timpani with feet comfortably spread apart. Sitting on a stool will help the taller player to better position the arms properly and to work the pedals more efficiently.

Timpani Range

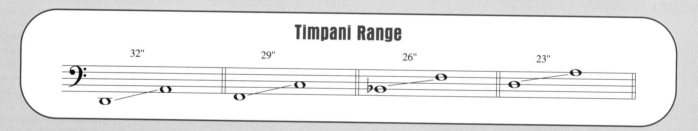

32"   29"   26"   23"

Advanced Care and Maintenance

- Use a cloth to keep the entire timpano clean and free of fingerprints, dust, and dirt.

- Keep the timpani covered when not in use.

- Keep the timpani mallets in a storage bag when not in use. Avoid touching the felt with your hands.

- Keep all objects off of the drum head; it's not a table.

- When you move the timpani, handle them only by the struts to avoid causing stress to the head.

- The average life of a timpani head is one to three years. Replace worn or damaged heads immediately.

Tuning

- Sound and listen to the tuning note for at least five seconds (pitch pipe).

- Sing or hum to match the pitch.

- Turn your head to keep the ear close to the timpani head.

- Think the pitch; don't hum while you pedal the drum.

- With the pedal in its lowest position, tap softly, once with the mallet and pedal-up (glissando) until you reach the desired pitch.

- Check the tuning with another soft mallet tap and adjust if necessary.

Please refer to the Art of Playing in Book One for more information.

The Art of Playing Keyboard Percussion
Instrument and Parts

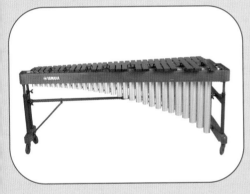

Orchestra Bells/Glockenspiel

The narrow metal tone bars are arranged in two rows similar to the piano keyboard. Play with plastic or hard rubber mallets. The bells sound two octaves higher than written.

History

- The Orchestra bells (glockenspiel) are thought to have descended from the bell lyre used by European marching bands of the nineteenth century.

- Paul Dukas wrote for the glockenspiel in his work, *The Sorcerer's Apprentice*, in 1897.

Xylophone

The narrow, thick wood or synthetic tone bars are arranged in two rows similar to the piano keyboard. Play with hard rubber mallets. The xylophone sounds one octave higher than written.

History

- Early forms of the xylophone can be traced back to 2000 B.C. in China.

- European folk musicians played the xylophone in the early part of the sixteenth century.

- The modern xylophone was popularized in North America by the migration of European musicians at the end of the nineteenth century.

- The xylophone grew in popularity with its acceptance as both a solo concert instrument and a novelty instrument in recordings, theater shows, and dance halls.

Marimba

The wide, thin wood or synthetic tone bars are arranged in two rows similar to the piano keyboard. Play with yarn or hard rubber mallets. The marimba sounds as written.

History

- The marimba is a descendant of the primitive xylophone brought to Central America by African slaves in the seventeenth century.

- Resonators were added underneath the wood slats, which were later arranged in two rows and tuned to accommodate Western-trained musicians.

Vibraphone/Vibes

The wide, thin metal tone bars are arranged in two rows similar to the piano keyboard. Play with yarn mallets. A dampening bar controls the sustain with the use of a foot pedal. The vibraphone sounds as written.

History

- The vibraphone was introduced to the public by several U.S. manufacturers in the first part of the twentieth century.

- A motor was added to rotate discs under each bar that created a vibrato effect. A pedal-operated dampening bar controlled the sustain.

Advanced Care and Maintenance

- Use a cloth to keep the entire instrument clean and free of fingerprints, dust, and dirt.

- Avoid using furniture polish on wood tone bars as it leaves a residue.

- Keep all objects off of the bars; it's not a table.

Storage Procedure

1. Keep the keyboard percussion instruments covered when not in use.
2. Store your mallets in a bag with all of your sticks and accessories.

Setup Procedure

1. All keyboard instruments should be flat and parallel to the floor.

2. Many keyboards have height-adjustable frames or stands. The height should be adjusted to waist level or slightly below.

Please refer to the Art of Playing in Book One for more information.

The Art of Playing Hand (Crash) Cymbals

History

1. Cymbals are curved metal plates with a raised center area.

2. Cymbals are one of the oldest known percussion instruments and first appeared in the Middle East as far back as 2500 B.C.

3. They were introduced to the Western orchestra through Turkish military bands of the seventeenth and eighteenth centuries.

Advanced Care and Maintenance

- Use a dry cloth or a mild solution of warm water and a little of dishwashing liquid to keep the cymbals clean and free of fingerprints and stick marks.

- Use a professional cymbal cleaner for deep cleaning.

- Store the cymbals in a separate padded bag and place them in a designated area on a shelf or in the percussion cabinet drawer. Avoid placing other objects on top of the instrument.

Play Position

Follow Thru Position

Soft Position

- To play a soft crash, place the cymbals parallel, 1" to 3" apart, and gently bring them together so that all edges touch at the same time.

Swish Position

- The swish technique creates a soft, sustained shimmer when the edge of one cymbal scrapes the grooves of another.

- Hold the left cymbal stationary at chest level.

- Place the edge of the right cymbal just above the inside bell area of the left cymbal.

- Slide the edge of the right cymbal upward in a smooth quick motion as you scrape the grooves.

- Start the scrape motion just before the written note of the swish so that it finishes on the beat.

Dampen Position

- Dampen the cymbals against your chest or shoulders to stop the sound.

Please refer to the Art of Playing in Book One for more information.

Rhythm Shake Position

- Rhythm shakes are performed with the tambourine in a vertical orientation
- Use your forearm to shake the tambourine from side to side to create the desired rhythm.
- Accents are created by striking the tambourine against the heel of the opposite hand.

Thumb Roll Play Position

- Grip the tambourine firmly in one hand with your thumb placed on the head and your fingers wrapped around the shell.
- Hold the tambourine in a vertical position at eye level to easily watch the tambourine, conductor, and the music.
- Straighten the thumb of your other hand and lightly rub the fleshy part of it around the edge of the of the tambourine head.
- Experiment with the angle of the tambourine and the amount of light, consistent pressure exerted on the head so that the maximum amount of jingle vibration is produced. Your thumb should be extended and the remaining fingers should be relaxed.
- A light coating of beeswax or rosin applied to the head will help create friction for your thumb to produce the roll. Moisten your thumb with a wet sponge to create additional friction. It may take repeated practicing and experimenting with the technique to achieve a consistent sound.

Knee/Fist Technique

- Use the knee/fist technique for fast and loud passages.
- Raise the knee of either leg by placing a foot on a chair.
- Hold the tambourine firmly in one hand in a horizontal orientation with the tambourine head side facing the floor.
- Strike the head alternately between your knee and closed fist of the opposite hand with a rapid motion of your forearm.
- Keep your wrist from flexing.
- Match the volume and tone of each strike from the knee and fist.
- Plan ahead to ensure that the tambourine is prepared with the correct orientation for playing with the head side down. If necessary, play the last stroke of a previous passage with a quick flip to turn over the tambourine to the correct orientation.

Finger/Rim Technique

- Use the finger/rim technique for fast and soft passages.
- Raise the knee of either leg by placing a foot on a chair.
- With the tambourine head side facing the floor, rest the tambourine securely on the elevated thigh with the forearms of both hands on the rim. The tambourine should extend just past the knee.
- Use one or more fingertips to play the rhythms on the rim; the more fingers, the more volume you will get. Louder passages may be played directly on the head with more fingers added.
- Use just enough arm pressure to keep the tambourine balanced while you play.
- Play directly over a jingle to get the clearest sound.
- The tambourine should be placed on a padded surface with the correct head orientation to make its pickup and replacement as silent as possible.

Please refer to the Art of Playing in Book One for more information.

The Art of Playing Bongos

Setup Procedure

1. Although bongos are traditionally played with the hands in a seated position, they can also be attached to a stand and played with snare drum sticks.

2. The drums should be flat and parallel to the floor. Adjust the stand to bring the top head to approximately waist level or slightly below.

3. The high drum may be placed on either the player's right or left to best accommodate the music.

History

1. Bongos are a small pair of high-pitched drums traditionally played with the hands.

2. They are traditionally played with the hands in a seated position, although they may also be attached to a stand and played with hands, sticks, or mallets.

3. Bongos originated in Cuba, where they provided accompaniment in small musical ensembles.

Rest Position

Ready Position

Open Tone Play Position

Muffled Tone Play Position

Rest Position
- The drums should be flat and parallel to the floor. Adjust the stand to bring the top head to approximately waist level if using sticks or slightly higher if playing with hands.
- Traditionally, right-handed players place the larger drum on their right. However, the larger drum may be placed on either the player's right or left to best accommodate the music.

Ready Position
- The shoulders are relaxed with the elbows away from the body and the forearms positioned horizontally.
- The fingers should be stretched and held close together without being stiff as they point towards the center of the drum.

Open Tone Play Position
- For open tones, the proper playing area is at the edge of each drum.
- Use a wrist motion, similar to using sticks on a snare drum, and play with relaxed arms.
- Strike the head flat with one-half the length of the four fingers on each hand.
- The fingers should immediately bounce off the head after each stroke.
- A quick, relaxed motion produces the clearest tone.

Muffled Tone Play Position
- For muffled tones, the proper playing area is near the center of each drum.
- Strike with head with the four fingertips of each hand.
- The fingers should remain on the head, momentarily, after each stroke.

Advanced Care and Maintenance

- Use a cloth to keep the entire drum clean and free of fingerprints, dust, and dirt.
- Keep all objects off of the drum head; it's not a table.
- The average life of a drum head is one year. Replace worn or damaged heads immediately.
- A small dab of lithium grease or lubrication should be applied to the tension rods when the heads are replaced.

The Art of Playing Triangle

History

1. The triangle is a steel rod that is bent in the shape of a triangle, with an open end, and struck with a thin metal beater.

2. It produces a bell-like tone with bright overtones of indefinite pitch.

3. Triangles of varias sizes volved from an ancient Egyptian instrument, the sistrum, and was introduced to the Western orchestra through Turkish military bands of the seventeenth and eighteenth centuries.

Advanced Care and Maintenance

- Store the triangle and accessories in a designated area on a shelf or in the percussion cabinet drawer. Avoid placing other objects on top of the instrument.

Rest Position

- The triangle may be clipped to the music stand to accommodate quick instrument changes or during rapid passages played with two beaters.

Ready Position

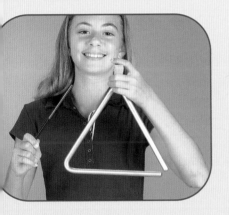

- The triangle should be suspended from a triangle clip with a thin piece of nylon line.

- Hold the clip comfortably in one hand so that your fingers can be used for muffling.

- Hold the triangle at eye level to easily watch the triangle, conductor, and the music.

- Hold the triangle beater near the end.

Play Position

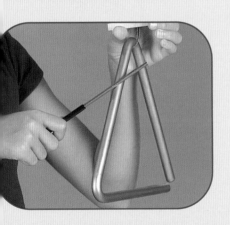

- Strike the triangle on the side directly opposite the open end or on the bottom.

- Play with a shorter stroke near the tip of the beater for a soft, delicate sound.

- Play with a longer stroke near the center of the beater for a louder, more colorful sound.

- A good triangle has a multitude of playing areas that will yield a variety of tones. Experiment with different playing areas and different size beaters to become familiar with all the sounds available.

Rolls Position

- Rolls are produced by rapidly moving the beater between the sides of one of the closed corners.

- To play a triangle roll, rapidly move the beater between the sides of the bottom closed corner.

- Change the angle of the beater as you roll to produce the most complex tone quality.

- Use a small portion of the corner and play at the tip of the beater to produce a soft roll. Move towards the center of the beater and cover more area as you increase volume.

- Fast, even rolls produce the most resonant sound.

Creative Tools of Music

Review

Anacrusis—one or more notes that come before the first full measure

Chorale—a slow, "hymn-like" composition

Dynamics—musical performance levels of loud and soft

Forte (*f*)—loud

Key Signature—flats and sharps placed immediately following the clef, indicating which notes are to be altered throughout the piece

Legato—play smooth and connected without interruption between the notes

March—music for a parade or procession

Mezzo Forte (*mf*)—medium loud

Mezzo Piano (*mp*)—medium soft

Phrase—a musical sentence or statement

Piano (*p*)—soft

Repeat Sign—a symbol that indicates to go back play the section of music again

Scale—a series of tones arranged in a set pattern from low to high or high to low

Staccato—play the note lightly and detached

Tempo—the speed of the beat

Tenuto—a symbol that means to play the note full va

Time Signature—a symbol placed at the beginning the staff where the top number indicates the numbe beats per measure and the bottom number what kin of note receives one beat

Unison (Unis.)—all performers sound the same no

New

Scale-Degree Numbers—signify the order in whic the pitches occur in a scale

1 Concert B♭ Pentascale Warm-Up

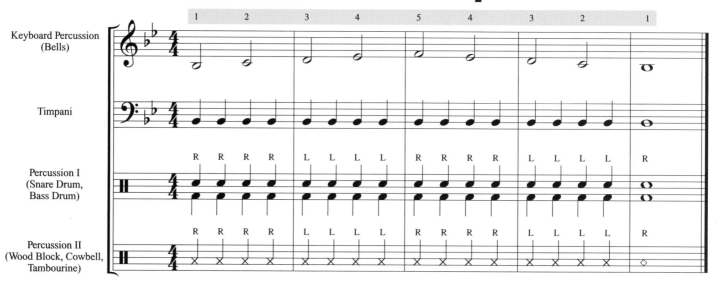

2 Rhythm Review

3 March Ionian CD:1

4 Concert B♭ Major Scale

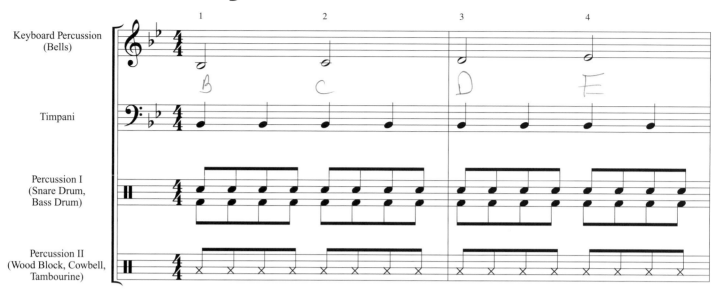

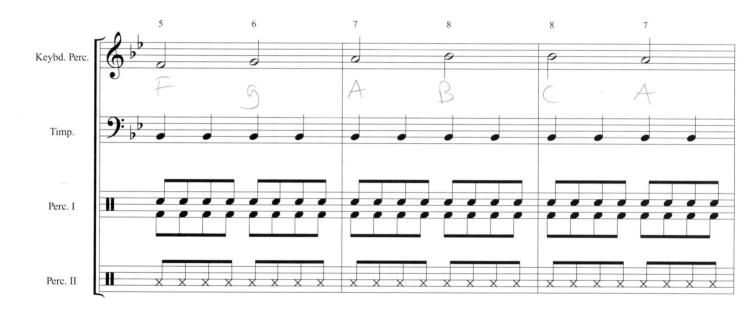

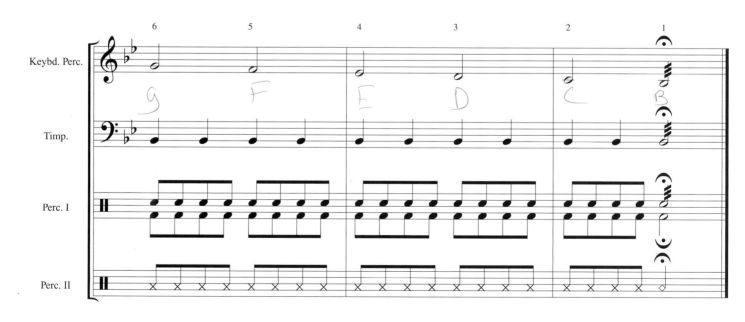

5 *Expressive Chorale*

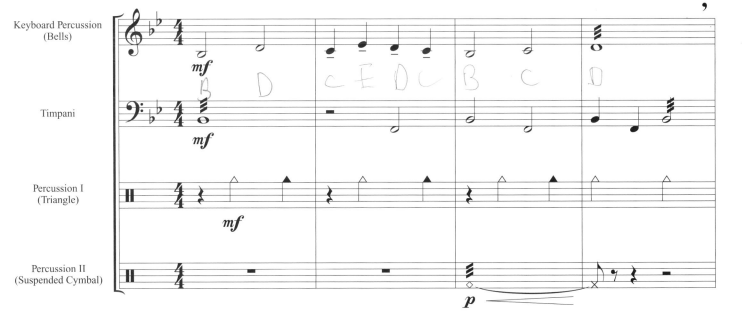

6 *The Merry-Go-Round Broke Down*

Words and Music by
CLIFF FRIEND and DAVE FRANKLIN

This Arrangement © 2005 WARNER BROS. INC.   All Rights Reserved

7 **Louie, Louie** CD :2

Rock!

By RICHARD BERRY

8 Manhattan Beach

CD :3

March

JOHN PHILIP SOUSA, U.S.A.

9 *Roll On, Dude!*

Rock & "Roll"

Band @ Home

LESSON 1

1. Prepare your instruments to play in class in our next meeting.

2. Be sure you have all the supplies necessary to play your instruments.

3. Remember to bring your stick bag or case and all implements to class.

LESSON 2

1. Practice "Rhythm Review" on each scale degree.

2. Perform "March Ionian" with the accompaniment track.

3. Practice Stroke Dexterity Exercises #1–10 using full strokes at a steady tempo.

LESSON 3

1. Practice "Rhythm Review" on each scale degree.

2. Improvise a four-note pattern using the first three scale degrees of the concert B♭ scale.

3. Perform "Louie, Louie" with the accompaniment track.

4. Practice Stroke Dexterity Exercises #11–20 using full strokes at a steady tempo.

5. Write a paragraph about all the places you heard music while on school break. This will be checked for completion at the beginning of our next class.

LESSON 4

1. Practice the concert B♭ major scale using different rhythms on each scale degree.

2. Perform "Manhattan Beach" and "Louie, Louie" with the accompaniment tracks for your family.

3. Review the Flam and practice the Five- and Nine-Stroke Rolls in both open and closed style. Always practice your rudiments slow-fast-slow. Start at a slow speed, gradually move to your fastest controlled tempo, and then gradually move back to slow. Each slow-fast-slow should take one minute.

4. Create an eight-pitch scale-degree composition using only the first five notes of the concert B♭ major scale. On a piece of paper, notate the composition, which may be performed by the class at our next meeting.

19

Creative Tools of Music

Review

1st and 2nd Endings—play the 1st ending, repeat the section and play only the 2nd ending the second time

Accent (>)—play the note with more emphasis

Allegro—fast tempo

Andante—moderately slow (walking) tempo

Divisi (Div.)—divide into two or more parts

Duet—a piece of music with two interacting parts

Moderato—moderate or medium tempo

Ostinato—a repeated melodic or rhythmic pattern

Syncopation—rhythm with the emphasis or stress on a weak beat or weak portion of a beat

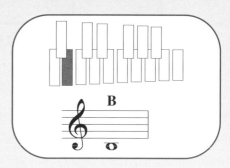

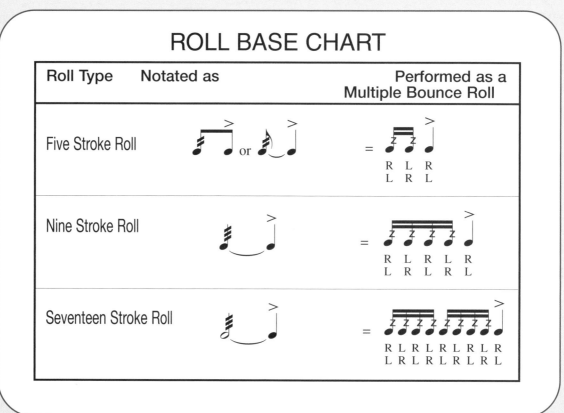

ROLL BASE CHART

Double Paradiddle

R L R L R R L R L R L L

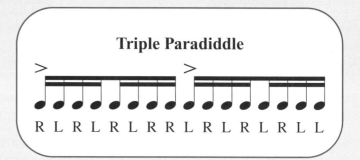

Triple Paradiddle

R L R L R L R R L R L R L R L L

10 *Back to Home*

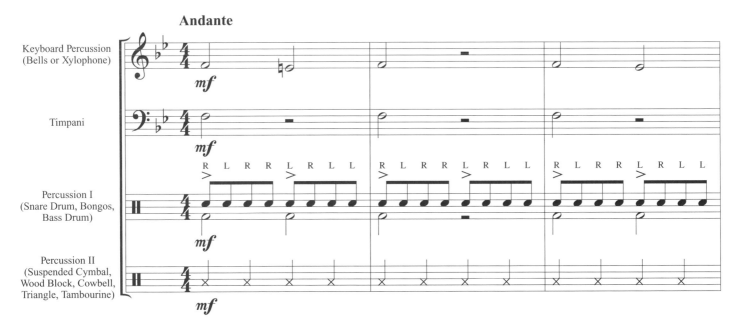

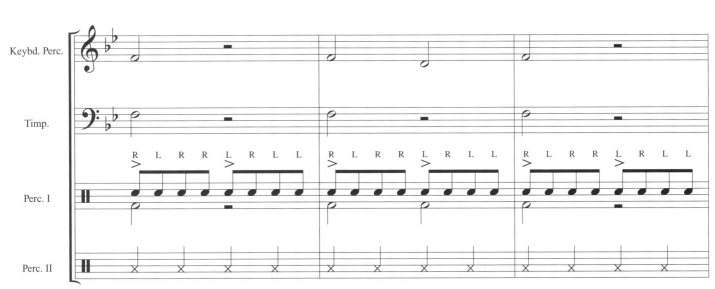

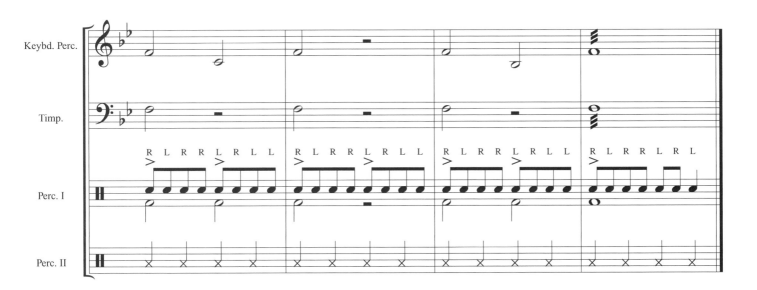

11 *Windsor Hills Chorale*

12 *Happy Birthday to You!* CD :4

Words and Music by
MILDRED J. HILL and PATTY S. HILL

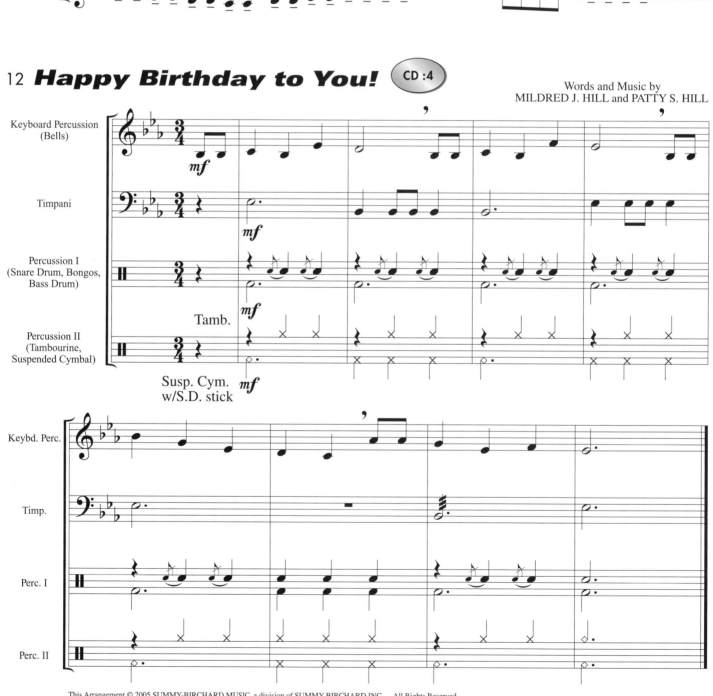

13 *The Marine's Hymn*

Music based on a theme by JACQUES OFFENBACH, France
Words attributed to COL. HENRY C. DAVIS, U.S.A.

14 *Matchmaker, Matchmaker*

Lyrics by SHELDON HARNICK
Music by JERRY BOCK

15 *The Yellow Rose of Texas* CD :5

Traditional, U.S.A.

16 Concert C Major Scale

17 Long Time No "C"

18 Theme From Ice Castles (Through the Eyes of Love)

CD :6

Music by MARVIN HAMLISCH
Lyrics by CAROLE BAYER SAGER

ine 18 continued

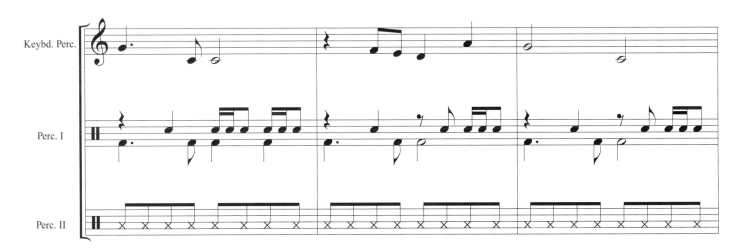

19 *El Capitan*

JOHN PHILIP SOUSA, U.S.A.

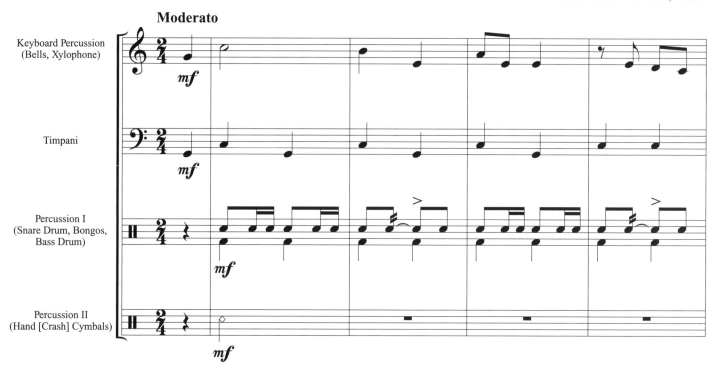

ine 19 continued

Band @ Home

LESSON 1

1. Warm up on long tones keeping each note steady for 9 counts.

2. Play the "The Marine's Hymn" and "Happy Birthday to You!" for your family and friends.

3. Practice the Paradiddle slow-fast-slow and Stroke Dexterity Exercises #1–20 at a variety of dynamic levels.

LESSON 2

1. Compose a new four measure scale degree composition. Create a one measure ostinato as an accompaniment.

2. Practice "The Yellow Rose of Texas" with the accompaniment track.

3. Practice the Double Paradiddle slow-fast-slow, and continue to review Stroke Dexterity Exercises #1–20.

LESSON 3

1. Practice singing and playing the new note concert B.

2. Perform "Theme From Ice Castles (Through the Eyes of Love)" with the accompaniment.

3. Continue to practice Stroke Dexterity Exercises #1–20.

4. Practice the Single, Double, and Triple Paradiddles slow-fast-slow.

UNIT 3

The Art of Playing Timbales

History

1. "Timbales" is the name for a pair of single-headed drums attached to a stand that are traditionally played with special thin timbale sticks or hand strokes. A modern timbale set-up often includes cymbals, wood blocks, and cowbells.

2. Timbales originated in Cuba, where they are a descendant of European orchestral timpani.

Advanced Care and Maintenance

- Use a dry cloth to keep the entire drums clean and free of fingerprints, dust, and dirt.

- Keep all objects off of the drum heads; they are not tables.

- The average life of a plastic drum head is one year. Replace worn or damaged heads immediately.

- A small dab of lithium grease or lug lubrication should be occasionally applied to the tension rods to aid in tuning.

Tuning

- The smaller timbale head should be tensioned until a natural rebound of the stick feels comfortable. The larger drum should be tuned about an interval of a fourth lower in pitch.

- Although there are a wide variety of tones that can be produced on timbales, they can be played on the heads like concert toms or on the sides of the shells (cascara). Rim shots are also used in traditional playing.

Rest Position

- The drums should be flat and parallel to the floor. Adjust the stand to bring the top head to approximately waist level.

- Traditionally, right-handed players place the larger drum on the left. However, the larger drum may be placed on either your right or left to best accommodate the music.

- The basic matched grip is the same as that for snare drum.

Ready Position

- Use the same ready position as that for the concert toms or snare drum.

Play Position

- Use the same strike technique as that for concert toms or snare drum.

Rim Shot Play Position

- A traditional rim shot is produced by simultaneously striking the rim and the timbale head with the end of a stick.

Cascara Play Position

- Strike the shell (cascara) with either or both sticks by pressing the shaft of the stick into the shell to achieve a non-ringing (dead) sound.

- It is helpful to point the index finger along the shaft of the stick to accommodate the "dead-stroke" technique.

The Art of Playing Claves

Setup Procedure

- Place the claves on a padded surface for easy access.

Ready Position

- Hold the clave at eye level so that you can easily watch it, the conductor, and the music.

- Hold the other clave near the end.

- Hold one clave gently with the fingertips of one hand to form a trough underneath. The clave should rest lightly in your hand so that it makes the most resonant sound possible.

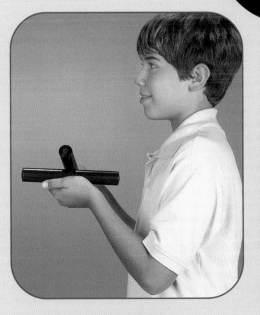

Play Position

- Using a wrist stroke similar to playing the snare drum, strike the clave in the middle with the other clave to produce a piercing, resonant tone.

- Experiment with the playing area to find the exact "sweet spot" of the claves.

Creative Tools of Music

Review

Slur—a curved line placed above or below two or more pitches, indicating that they are to be performed smoothly and connected

New

Theme—the main idea in a composition
Variation—a restatement that retains some features of the original idea or theme

Rim Shot

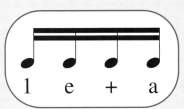

1   e   +   a

6 = beats in a measure
4 = type of note/rest that receives one beat

Drag

L L R   R R L

Single Drag Tap

L L R   L   R R L   R

20 *Lip Slurs*

Moderato

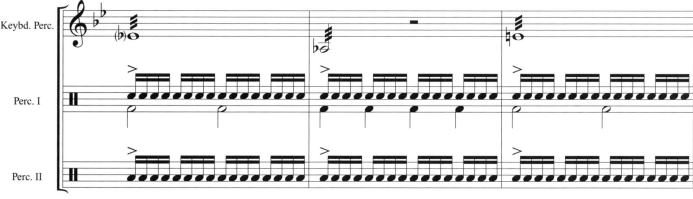

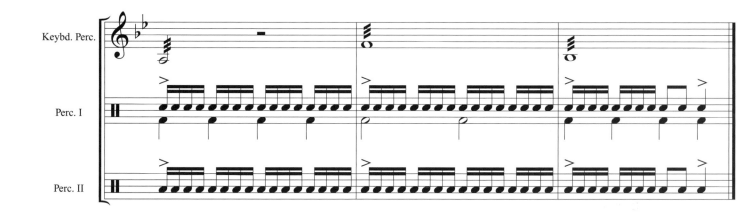

UNIT 3

21 *Isolation*

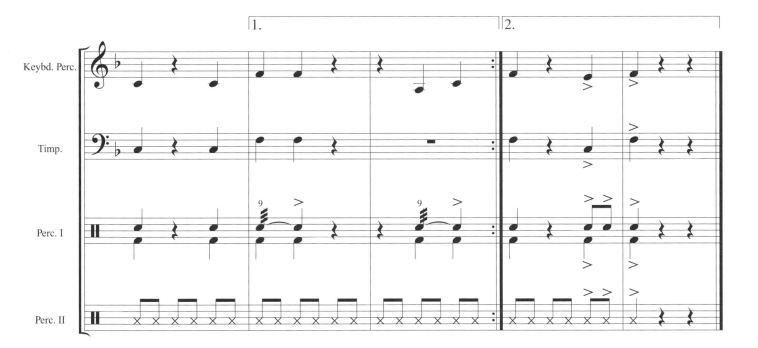

33

UNIT 3

22 *Short and Sweet*

23 *Return of the Lip Slurs*

24 Rockin' Rolling Sixteenths CD :7

25 *Twinkle Variation I*

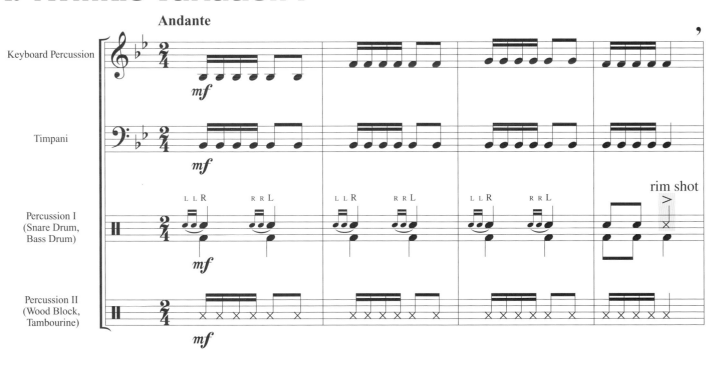

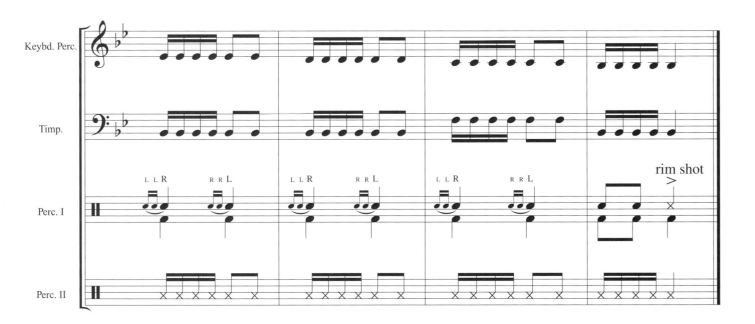

26 Happy Birthday to You!

Words and Music by
MILDRED J. HILL and PATTY S. HILL

27 Down and Up

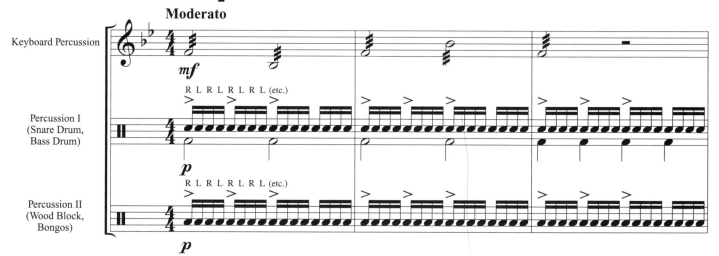

ine 27 continued

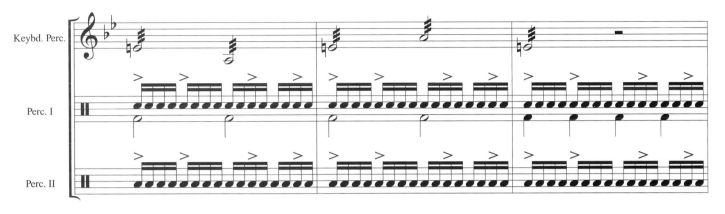

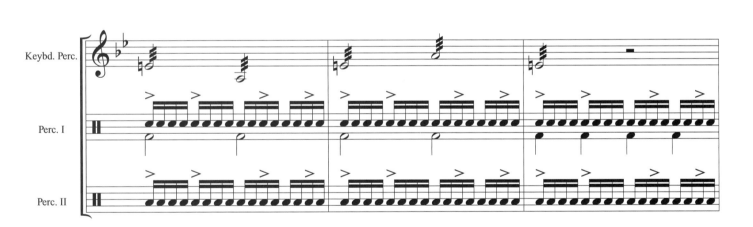

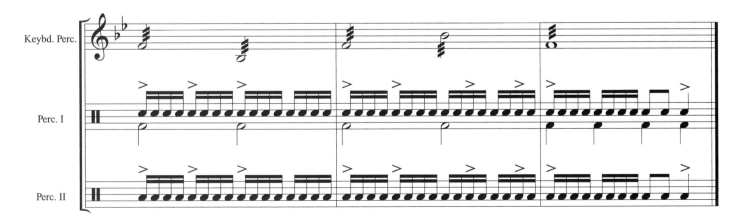

28 Sixteenth Extension

29 Twinkle Variation II

30 *Tongue Twister* CD :8

Band @ Home

LESSON 1

1. Look ahead and practice "Rockin' Rolling Sixteenths."

2. Your practice session should now include Accent Dexterity Exercises #1–4.

LESSON 2

1. Practice "Rockin' Rolling Sixteenths" with the accompaniment track and "Happy Birthday to You!" in the 6/4 time signature.

2. Practice the Drag rudiments slow-fast-slow in both open and closed style and Accent Dexterity Exercises #1–4.

LESSON 3

1. Review "Twinkle Variation I & II" and "Tongue Twister," gradually increasing the tempo.

2. Review Accent Dexterity Exercises #1–4 with a crescendo and decrescendo.

The Art of Playing Castanets

History

1. Castanets are a pair of spoon-shaped, hard-wood shells, strung together, and clapped together to produce a sharp, high-pitched sound.

2. The traditional construction material commonly used is ebony or rosewood, but it is also common to find hard synthetic castanets in school situations.

3. Castanets are traditionally strung around the thumb and played by dancers with highly-developed finger technique. Concert percussionists use either a paddle castanet (mounted on a handle) or a machine castanet (spring mounted on a board).

4. Castanets are most often associated with the music and dance of Spain and Latin American countries.

Advanced Care and Maintenance

• Use a dry cloth to keep the castanets clean and free of fingerprints, dust, and dirt.

• Keep the castanets stored in a designated area on a shelf or in the percussion cabinet drawer and avoid placing other objects on top of the instrument.

Rest Position

• The paddle castanets should be placed on a padded surface to make the pickup and replacement as silent as possible

Ready Position

• Hold the paddles at chest level, parallel to the floor.

Play Position

• Make a quick downward wrist stroke in the air to sound the castanets.

• Rhythms are played using single alternating strokes

Rapid Play Position

• Place the foot on a chair and play the castanets against the upper leg for rapid passages.

Rolls Play Position

• Rolls are played with the clappers turned perpendicular to the floor in a rapid side-to-side motion.

The Art of Playing Congas

History

1. "Congas" is the name for a set of single-headed barrel drums manufactured in three traditional sizes and used to play Latin music: quinto (small drum with 11" head), conga (medium drum with 11"–11 3/4" head), and tumbadora (large drum with 12"–12 1/2" head).

2. Congas are traditionally played with the hands in a seated position, although they may also be attached to a stand and played with hands, sticks, or mallets.

3. They originated in Cuba, where they are a direct descendent of African drums.

Advanced Care and Maintenance

- Use a cloth to keep the entire drum clean and free of fingerprints, dust, and dirt. Wipe excess dirt off the conga heads with a clean, damp cloth.

- To lengthen the life of natural skin heads, lower the pitch of the drums after playing them. The average life of a plastic drum head is one year. Replace worn or damaged heads immediately.

- Keep all objects off of the drum heads; they are not tables.

- A small dab of lithium grease or lug lubrication should be occasionally applied to the tension rods to aid in tuning.

Tuning

- Congas should be tensioned high enough to achieve an open tone that clearly projects. A pair of drums should be tuned about the interval of a fourth apart in pitch.

- There are a wide variety of tones that can be produced on congas. Two basic hand strokes are the "Open Tone" and the "Bass Tone".

Rest Position

- The drums should be flat and parallel to the floor. Adjust the stand to bring the top head to approximately waist level or slightly below.

- When using a pair of congas, right-handed players traditionally place the larger drum on the right. When additional drums are added, they are placed on either the player's right or left to best accommodate the music

Ready Position

- Relax the shoulders with the elbows away from your body and your forearms positioned horizontally.

- Your fingers should be stretched and held close together without being stiff as they point towards the center of the drum.

Open tone Position

- For open tones, the proper playing area is at the edge of each drum.

- Strike the head flat with the entire length of your four fingers on each hand, with the underside of your knuckles landing on the edge of the drum.

- Your thumb is held out to the side to avoid striking the rim.

- Your fingers should immediately bounce off the head after each stroke, producing a resonant open tone.

- A quick, relaxed motion produces the clearest tone.

Bass tone Position

- For bass tones, the proper playing area is at the center of each drum where the deepest tones are produced.

- Drop your entire hand (fingers, thumb, and palm strike simultaneously) on to the head.

- Your hand should remain relaxed on the head until the next stroke.

UNIT 4

Creative Tools of Music

Divisi (div.)—divide into two or more parts

D.S. al Fine—return to the sign and play to the fine

Tuning—adjustment of the instrument to match a given pitch

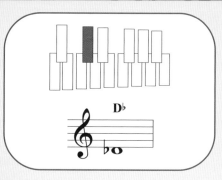

Dᵇ

Cross-stick Rim Shot

Up

Down

Lesson 25

31 *An Uphill Climb*

32 *Chordal Chorale*

44

33 *Las Mañanitas*

Traditional, Mexico

34 Guantanamera

CD :9

Original Words and Music by JOSÉ FERNANDEZ
Music adaptation by PETE SEEGER
Lyric adaptation by HECTOR ANGULO

Line 34 continued

35 *Jammin' on Concert D♭*

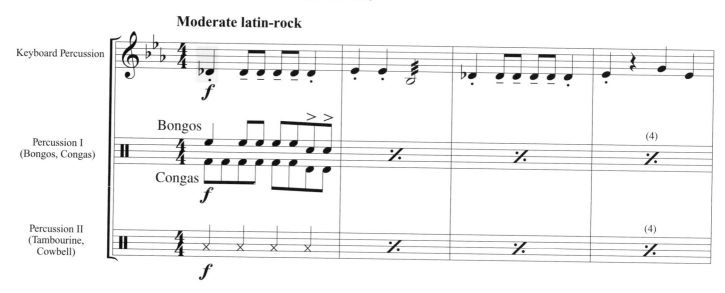

UNIT 4

36 **La Paloma**

SEBASTIAN YRADIER, Spain

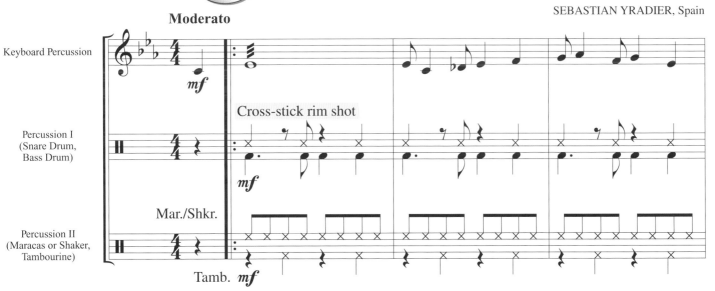

37 *F Stretch*

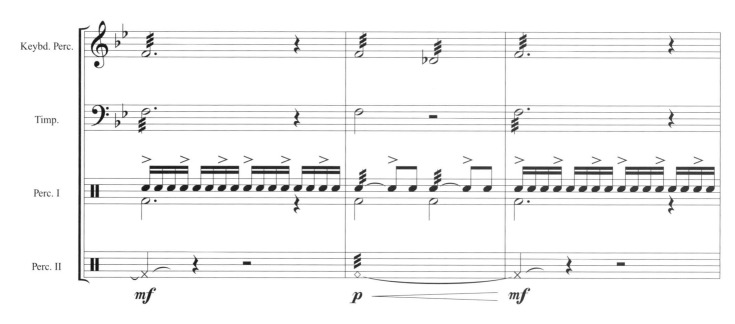

38 *Lady of Spain*

Words by ERELL REAVES
Music by TOLCHARD EVANS

39 *Sweet Sixteenths*

40 *Batman* CD :11

Words and Music by NEAL HEFTI

Band @ Home

LESSON 1

1. Perform "Guantanamera" with the accompaniment track for your family and friends.

2. Practice Accent Dexterity Exercises #5-8.

LESSON 2

1. Warm up carefully before each practice session.

2. Practice the new note concert D♭ and "Jammin' on Concert D♭."

3. Practice Accent Dexterity Exercises #5-8 and continue to review all of the rudiments you have learned so far. Maintain control as you practice each one slow-fast-slow.

LESSON 3

1. Perform "Batman" both with and without the accompaniment for your family and friends.

2. Practice the Lesson 25 rudiment slow-fast-slow in both closed and open styles, and Accent Dexterity Exercises #5–8.

Creative Tools of Music

New

Enharmonics—notes that are spelled differently on the staff, but sound the same
Folk Song—a song passed down from generation to generation that most people learn by hearing others sing or play it
Interval—the distance between two pitches
Simile—in the same style

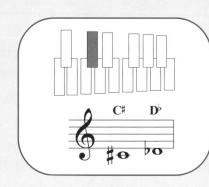

In $\frac{2}{2}, \frac{3}{2}, \frac{4}{2}$:

o = 2 beats

♩ = 1 beat

♪ = 1/2 beat

$\frac{4}{2}$ = beats in a measure
= half note/rest receives one beat

$\frac{3}{2}$ = beats in a measure
= half note/rest receives one beat

$\frac{2}{2}$ = beats in a measure
= half note/rest receives one beat

41 *Aura Lee Warm-Up*

Words by W.W. FOSDICK, U.S.A.
Music by GEORGE R. POULTON, U.S.A.

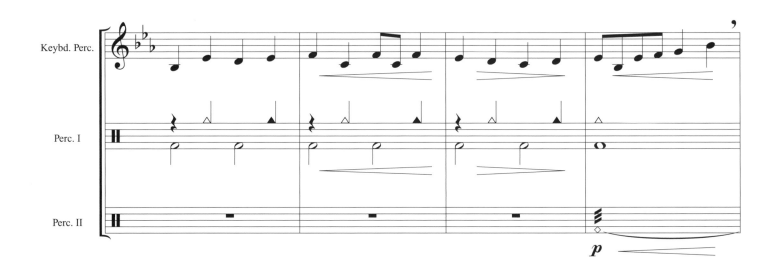

Line 41 continued

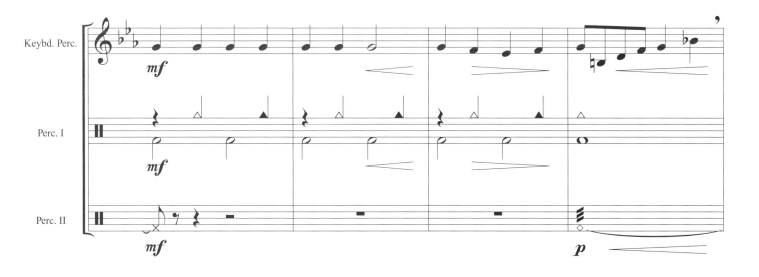

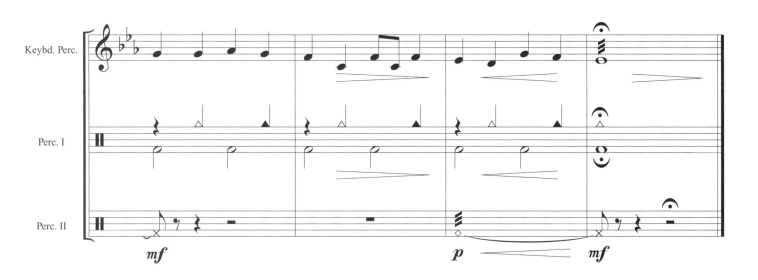

42 *My Old Kentucky Home*

STEPHEN FOSTER, U.S.A.

Rolls Position

43 *March Militaire*

Be prepared for you or your standmate to quickly turn the page.

Line 43 continued

line 43 continued

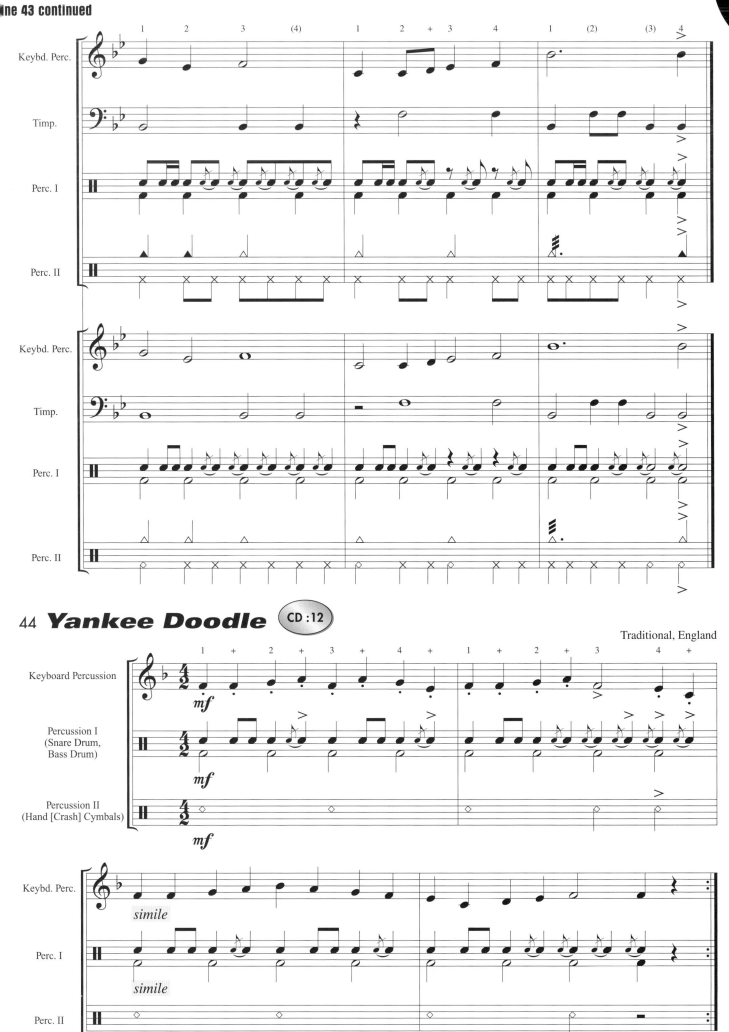

44 **Yankee Doodle** CD :12

Traditional, England

UNIT 5

45 *Concert B♭ Major Scale Warm-Up*

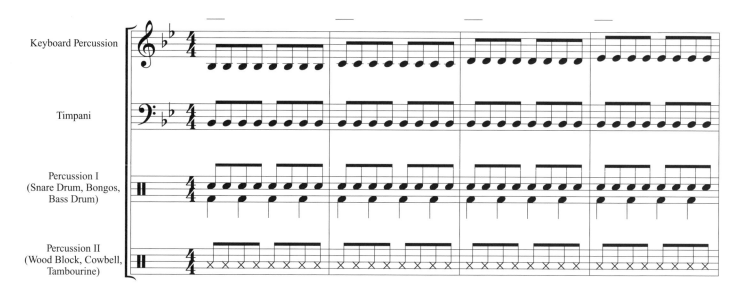

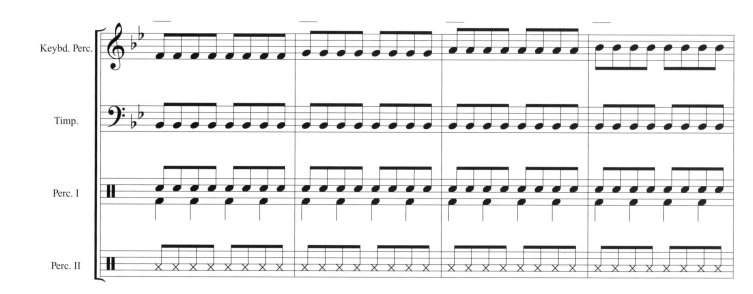

ne 45 continued

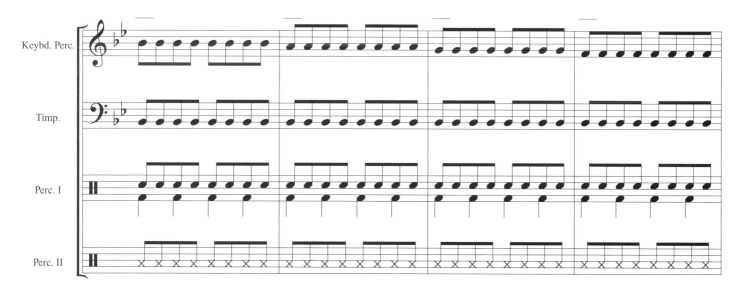

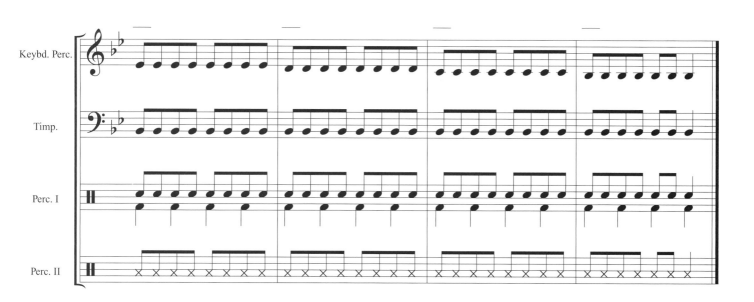

46 *Happy Birthday to You!*

Words and Music by
MILDRED J. HILL and PATTY S. HILL

line 46 continued

47 Manhattan Beach 4/2

JOHN PHILIP SOUSA, U.S.A.

March

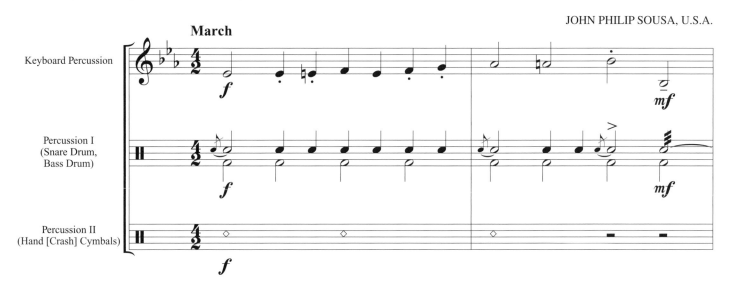

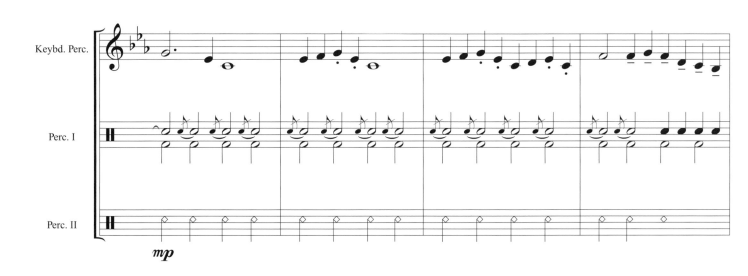

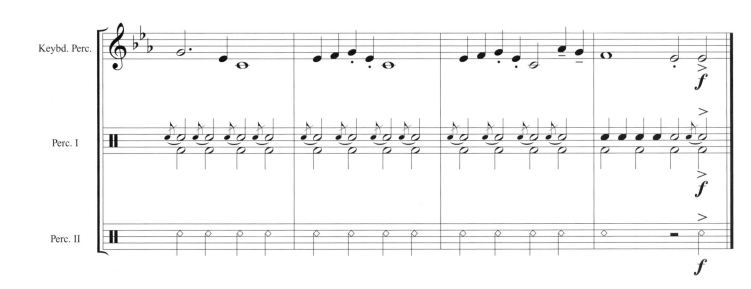

48 *Jingle Bells* CD:13

JAMES PIERPONT, U.S.A.

49 *Modern Enharmonics*

e 49 continued

Band @ Home

LESSON 1

1. Practice "Yankee Doodle" and then perform with the accompaniment track for your family and/or friends.

2. Ask your parents, family, or friends if they know a folk song. If so, ask them to sing it to you and share its role in history.

3. Practice Accent Dexterity Exercise #9.

LESSON 2

1. Practice "Happy Birthday to You!" in both the 3/4 and 3/2 time signatures. Be prepared to play it for your family or friends at the next birthday celebration.

2. Listen for music of different periods on the radio, television, or audio recording.

3. Practice Accent Dexterity Exercise #10.

LESSON 3

1. Perform "Jingle Bells" with and without the accompaniment track for your family and friends. Before you play the piece, be sure to inform them that you are now reading in both 2/2 and 2/4 time signatures.

2. Compose your own chant with neighboring scale degrees for our next class.

3. Practice your Accent Dexterity Exercises #9–10 and review all of the rudiments you have learned so far.

Creative Tools of Music

Crescendo, *Cresc.*—gradually get louder
Decrescendo, *Decresc.*—gradually get softer
Articulation—a slight interruption of the air stream with the tongue
Chromatic Scale—a scale made up of only half steps
Diminuendo, *Dim.*—gradually get softer
Half Steps—the distance between two adjacent notes
Pentascale—five note scale
Poco a poco—little by little

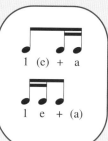

Flamacue

Sunday, Music in the Country,
by Raoul Dufy (1877–1953)

PORTRAIT

Henry Fillmore

Henry Fillmore was born in Cincinnati, Ohio, in 1881. Because his father was in the music publishing business, young Henry was exposed to music at a very early age. Henry Fillmore had a well-trained singing voice, and he sang in the choir. He spent time with the piano and mastered the flute, violin, and guitar. His fascination with the slide trombone led to intense study of the instrument and influenced many famous compositions in his later life.

Fillmore then began a career in circus music, playing in a circus band. After leaving the circus and working in his father's publishing business, he organized his own professional band. The Fillmore Band, which was the last in a long line of great professional bands of its type in America (the Sousa band had passed into history when Fillmore began his band), became immensely popular. Fillmore and his band entertained with a variety of musical styles. He often turned directly around to the audience and conducted the band, finishing numbers with long fermatas (holds or pauses), and demonstrating how much he enjoyed the audience's presence. Henry Fillmore was called "Showman Supreme."

Henry Fillmore's compositions are best known through his marches. They include "American We," "Men of Ohio," "His Honor," "The Footlifter," and "Military Escort." "Military Escort" has been called the best easy march ever composed. John Philip Sousa told Henry Fillmore that he wished Sousa's name were on this march. "Men of Ohio" was dedicated to President Warren G. Harding, who had played the alto horn in his high school band in Marion, Ohio.

50 Pentascale Warm-Up

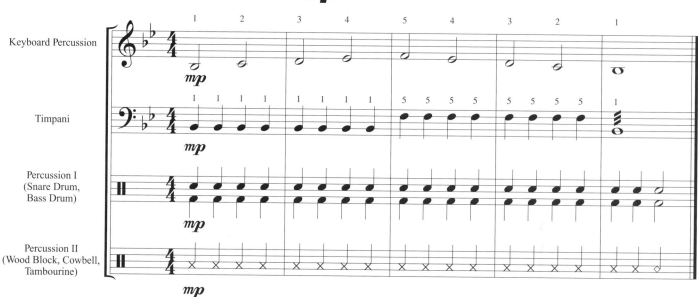

51 *Chromatic Warm-Up (Concert B♭)*

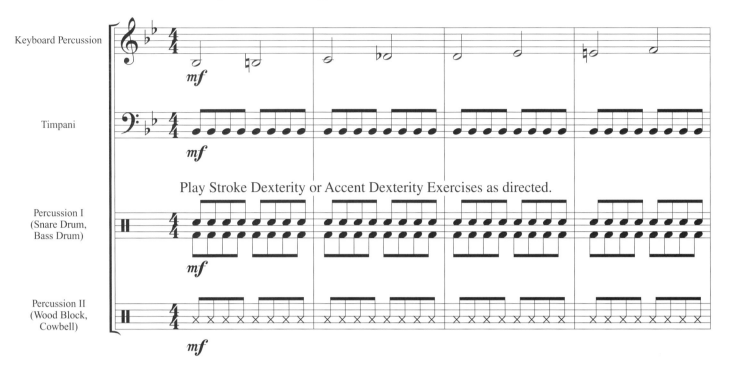

Play Stroke Dexterity or Accent Dexterity Exercises as directed.

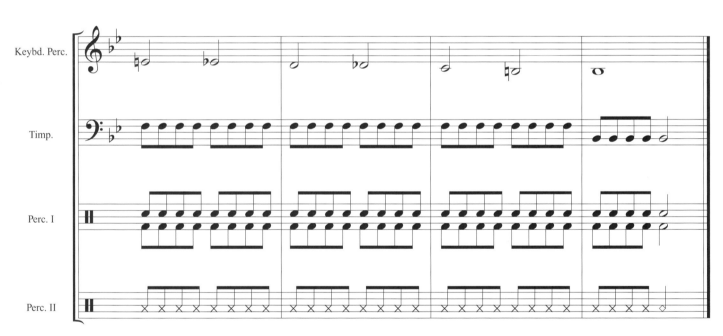

Rolls Play Position

52 *Flamacue March*

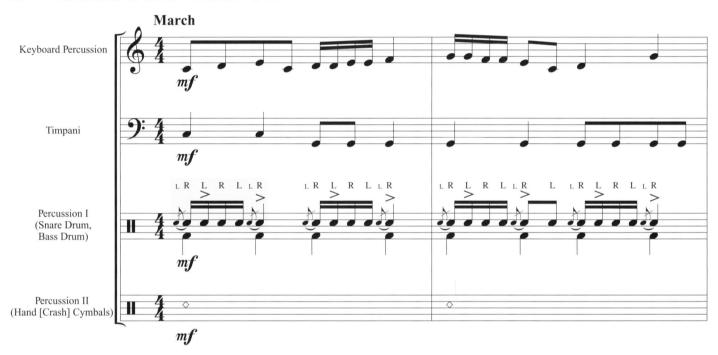

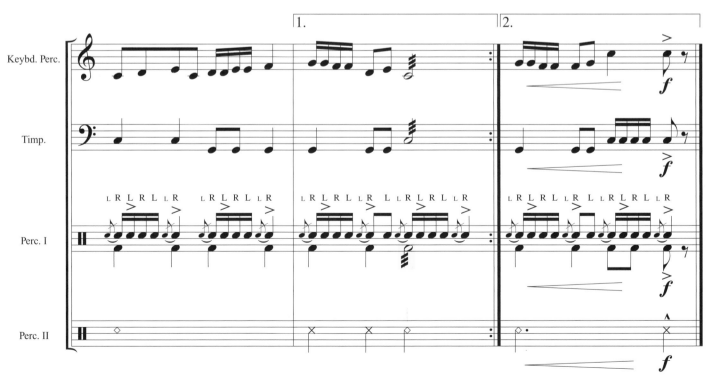

53 *Chromatics de la Cool* CD :14

54 *Star Chorale*

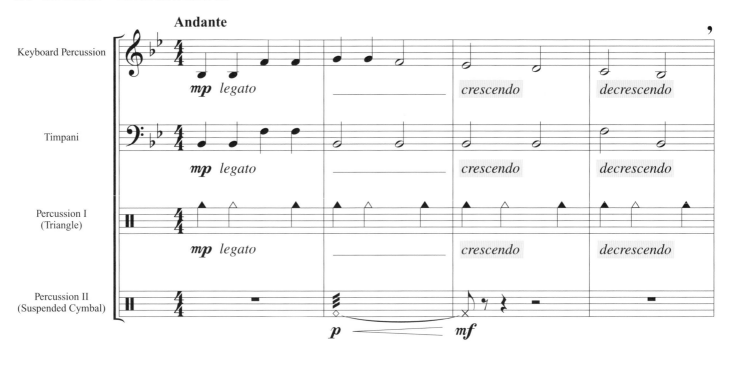

55 *Subdivide and Conquer!*

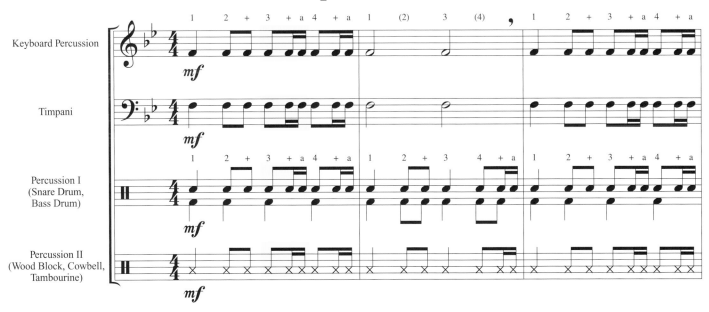

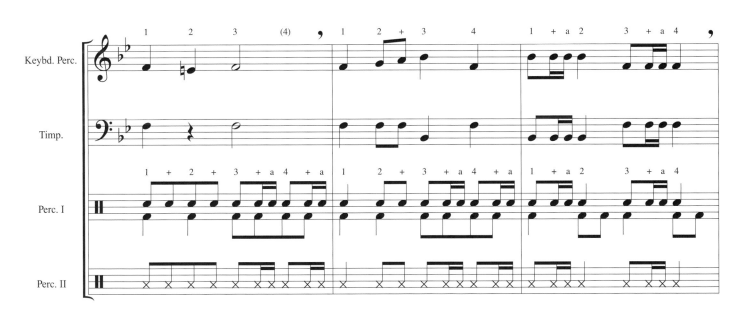

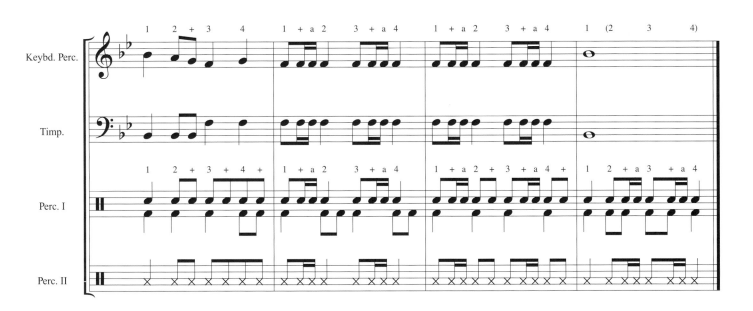

56 *Military Escort* CD :15

HAROLD BENNETT (HENRY FILLMORE), U.S.A.

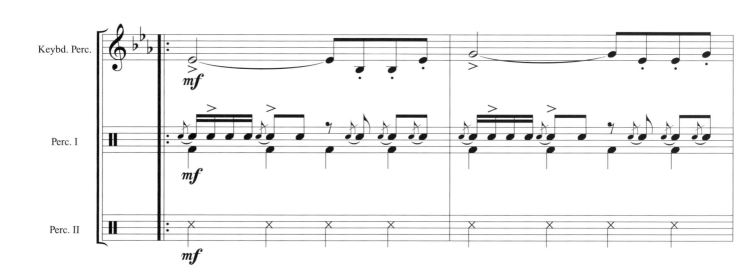

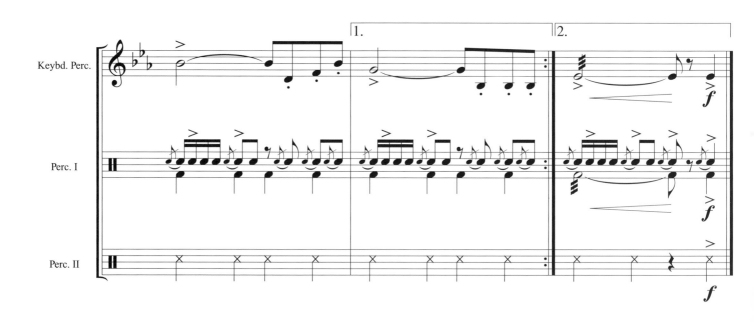

57 *Ragtime Rhythms* CD :16

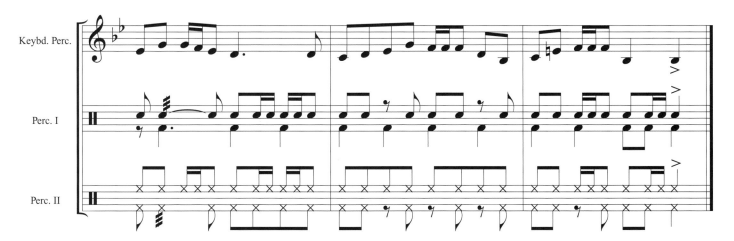

Band @ Home

LESSON 1

1. Play the "Pentascale Warm-Up" and "Chromatic Warm-Up (Concert B♭)" as part of your warm-up procedure.

2. Perform "Chromatics de la Cool" with and without the accompaniment tracks for your family and friends.

3. Practice the Flamacue slow-fast-slow and the Accent Dexterity Exercises #11–12.

LESSON 2

1. Practice "Pentascale Warm-Up" and "Star Chorale" as part of your warm-up procedure. Be sure to practice singing the interval of a fifth and checking your pitch with your instrument.

2. Perform "Ragtime Rhythms" with the accompaniment track for your family and friends.

3. Practice the Flamacue slow-fast-slow and the Accent Dexterity Exercises #11–12.

LESSON 3

1. Practice the "Pentascale Warm–Up" and "Star Chorale" as part of your warm-up procedure. Practice singing the intervals of a second and a fifth, checking the pitch with your instrument.

2. Continue practicing the Accent Dexterity Exercises #11–12 and the Flamacue slow-fast-slow.

3. Improvise your version of "Pentascale Improv" with CD :17. Be sure to try many rhythmic and pitch variations using the interval of a second.

CD :17

UNIT 7

Creative Tools of Music

Review

D.C. al Fine—return to the beginning and play to the fine

Fortissimo (**ff**)—very loud

Marcato—a style of playing where the notes are accented or stressed

Pianissimo (**pp**)—very soft

New Note: Concert G♭;

See the position chart in the back of this book

Concert Key	B♭	F	E♭	C	A♭	G
C Instruments	B♭	F	E♭	C	A♭	G
B♭ Instruments	C	G	F	D	B♭	A
E♭ Instruments	G	D	C	A	F	E
F Instruments	F	C	B♭	G	E♭	D

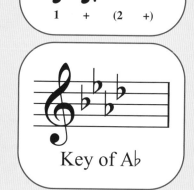

Key of A♭

PORTRAIT

Johann Sebastian Bach
(1685–1750)

Johann Sebastian Bach was one of the most important composers in European history. He was a church musician all of his life and people today still regularly sing and play his music in church. He did not play the piano until he was an old man, so most of his keyboard music was composed for the organ or clavichord, a very popular keyboard instrument during the Baroque era. The Baroque era style included much ornamentation that was added to clothing, furniture, and architecture. Baroque music also was very ornamented.

58 Dynamic Chorale

59 *March Marcato* CD :18

60 Camptown Races

Words and Music by STEPHEN FOSTER, U.S.A.

61 Concert A♭ Major Scale

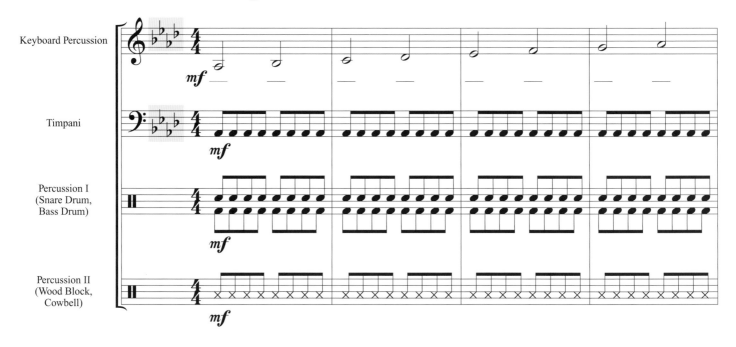

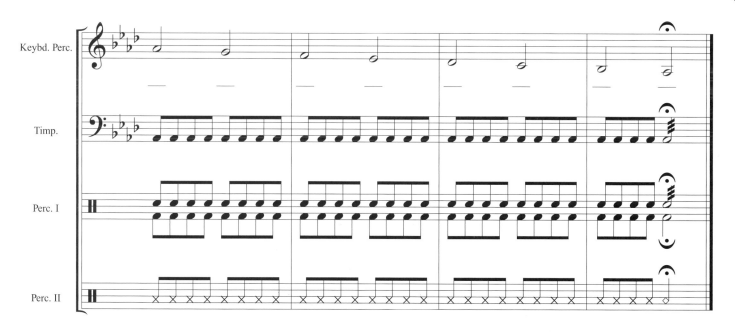

Line 61 continued

62 *Bach Chorale*

JOHANN SEBASTIAN BACH, Germany

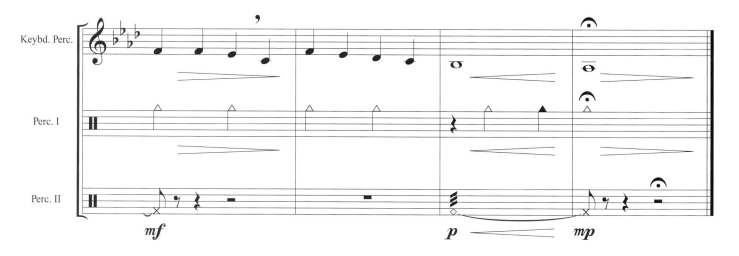

63 Bach Minuet

JOHANN SEBASTIAN BACH, Germany

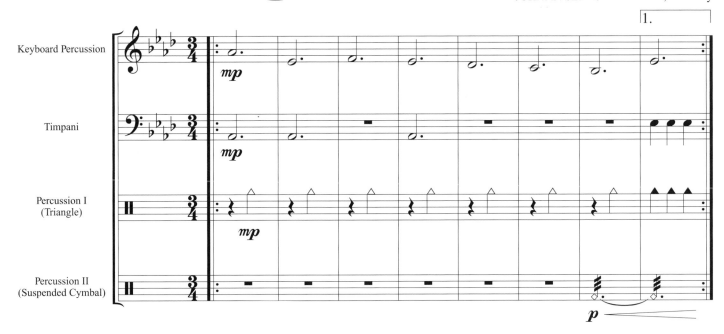

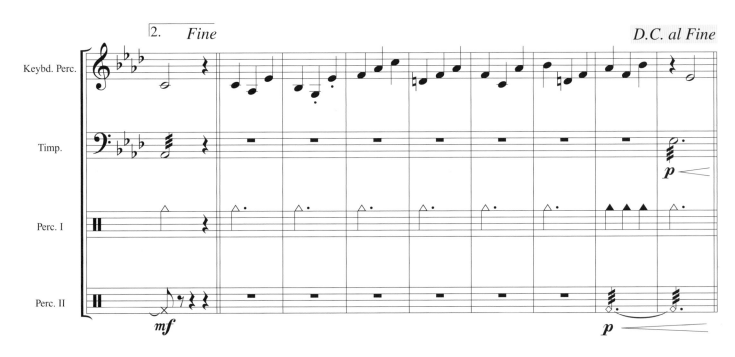

Thumb Roll Play Position

- Grip the tambourine firmly in one hand with your thumb placed on the head and your fingers wrapped around the shell.

- Hold the tambourine in a vertical position at eye level to easily watch the tambourine, conductor, and the music.

- Straighten the thumb of your other hand and lightly rub the fleshy part of it around the edge of the of the tambourine head.

- Experiment with the angle of the tambourine and the amount of light, consistent pressure exerted on the head so that the maximum amount of jingle vibration is produced. Your thumb should be extended and the remaining fingers should be relaxed.

- A light coating of beeswax or rosin applied to the head will help create friction for your thumb to produce the roll. Moisten your thumb with a wet sponge to create additional friction. It may take repeated practicing and experimenting with the technique to achieve a consistent sound.

64 **Tambourine Tango** CD :20

Knee/Fist Technique

- Use the knee/fist technique for fast and loud passages.
- Raise the knee of either leg by placing a foot on a chair.
- Hold the tambourine firmly in one hand in a horizontal orientation with the tambourine head side facing the floor.
- Strike the head alternately between your knee and closed fist of the opposite hand with a rapid motion of your forearm.
- Keep your wrist from flexing.
- Match the volume and tone of each strike from the knee and fist.
- Plan ahead to ensure that the tambourine is prepared with the correct orientation for playing with the head side down. If necessary, play the last stroke of a previous passage with a quick flip to turn over the tambourine to the correct orientation.

65 *Entry of the Gladiators* CD :21

JULIUS FUCIK, Czech Republic

ne 65 continued

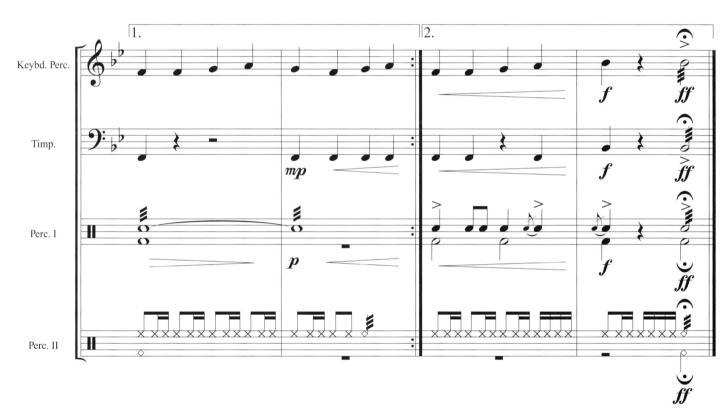

Band @ Home

LESSON 1

1. Create a scale-degree sequence and notate the scale-degree numbers on a piece of paper. Sing it and perform it on your instrument.

2. Play "Dynamic Chorale" and "March Marcato," using proper dynamic levels, tone quality, and playing style.

3. Practice Accent Dexterity Exercises #13–14.

LESSON 2

1. Practice the concert A♭ major scale.

2. Create a five-note composition in concert A♭ using scale-degree numbers. Notate it on the back of Worksheet #9. Use a minimum of two intervals of a third.

3. Play "Bach Minuet" for your family and friends.

4. Practice Accent Dexterity Exercises #13–14.

LESSON 3

1. Continue practicing the concert A♭ major scale, gradually increasing the tempo and varying the articulation with each repetition.

2. Play "Entry of the Gladiators" and "Tambourine Tango" for your family and friends with the accompaniment tracks.

3. Continue practicing Accent Dexterity Exercises #13–14, increasing the tempo as you gain proficiency.

UNIT 8 IS PRESENTED BY YOUR TEACHER

UNIT 9

The Art of Playing Ratchet

UNIT 8 IS PRESENTED BY YOUR TEACHE

Rest Position

- The standard ratchet can be held in one hand or mounted to the rim of a concert bass drum.

Ready Position

- Hold the leg of the ratchet in one hand at chest level.

Play Position

- The characteristic sound of the ratchet is a loud sustain, created by turning the handle with a smooth, consistent motion.

- Rhythms can be performed by making small, quick turns of the handle.

- Volume is increased by turning the handle more rapidly, and decreased by turning the handle slowly.

Advanced Care and Maintenance

- Place the ratchet in a designated area on a shelf or in the percussion cabinet drawer and avoid placing other objects on top of the instrument.

Creative Tools of Music

Key Change—a change from one key to another key in a piece of music, indicated by a new key signature

Lento—slow

Phrasing—the art of playing musical sentences or statements

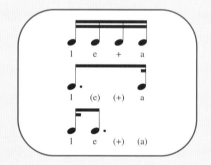

66 *Descending Echo Warm-Up*

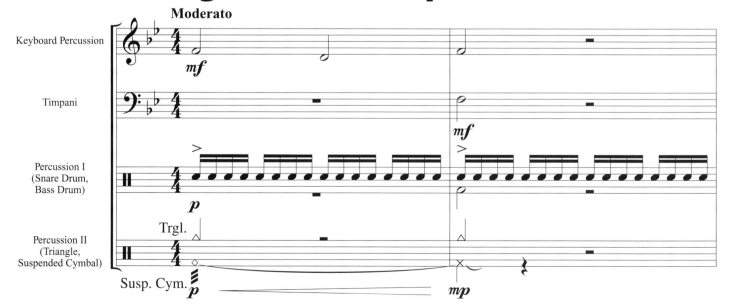

84

Ine 66 continued

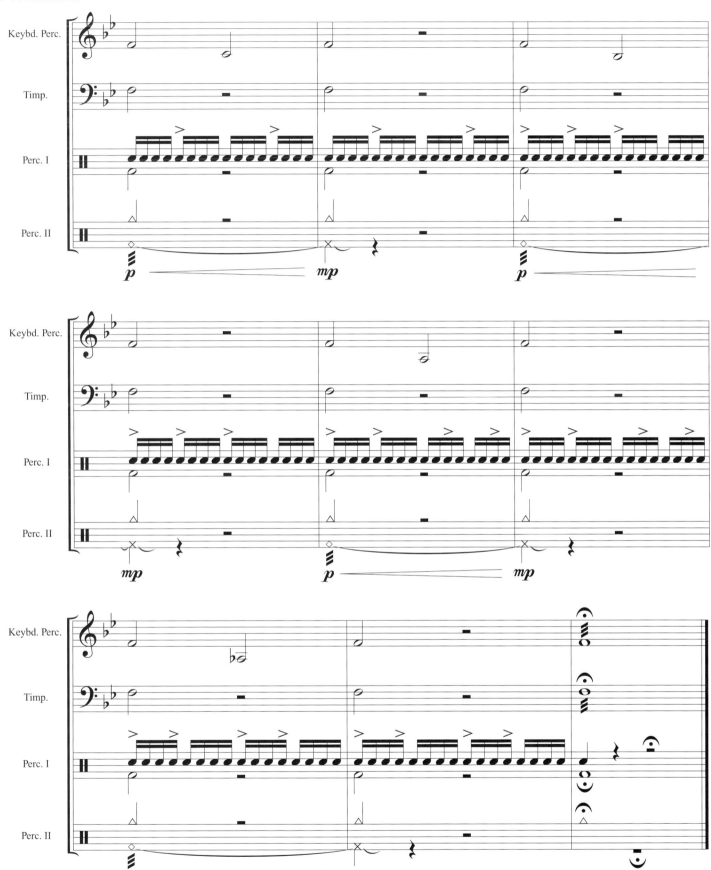

67 **Windsor Hills Chorale**

68 *On the Dot*

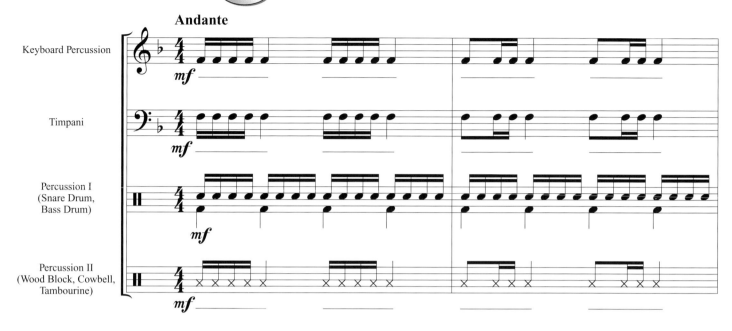

69 *Bamboo Fiah* CD :23

Folk Song, Guyana

ine 69 continued

70 ***The Imperial March*** CD :24
(Darth Vader's Theme)

Music by **JOHN WILLIAMS**

71 *Over the Rainbow* CD :25

Music by HAROLD ARLEN
Lyrics by E.Y. HARBURG

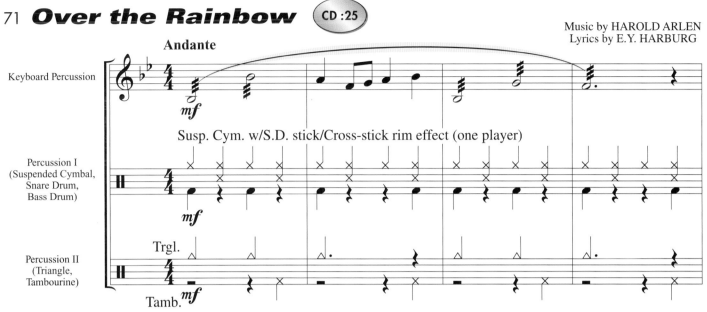

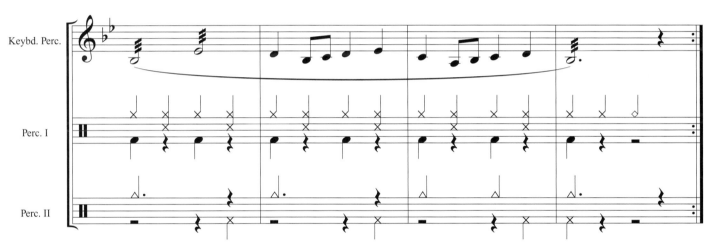

72 *Londonderry Air*

Traditional Air, Ireland

73 Reverse the Dot

74 Loch Lomond

Traditional, Scotland

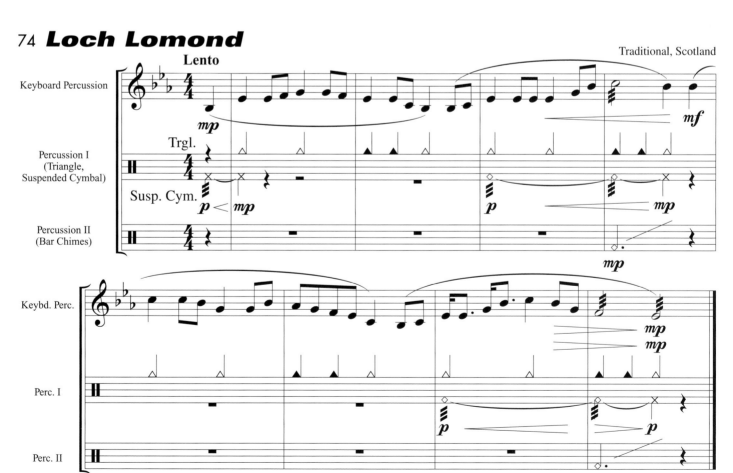

75 **Dry Bones** CD :26

Music by ROSAMOND JOHNSON
Words by JAMES WELDON JOHNSON

Keyboard Percussion

Percussion I
(Snare Drum,
Bass Drum)

Percussion II
(Suspended Cymbal,
Ratchet)

(Bundle sticks)

Ratchet

Susp. Cym.
w/S.D. stick

Keybd. Perc.

Perc. I

Perc. II

Keybd. Perc.

Perc. I

Perc. II

Keybd. Perc.

Perc. I

Perc. II

Band @ Home

LESSON 1

1. Play the dotted–eighth–sixteenth rhythm on a concert Bb major scale.

2. Perform "Bamboo Fiah" with the accompaniment track for your family and friends. Tell them about the country of Guyana.

3. Review the Accent Dexterity Exercises #1–5 at varying dynamic levels.

LESSON 2

1. Perform "Londonderry Air" and "Over the Rainbow" with correct phrasing for your family and friends.

2. Review the Accent Dexterity Exercises #6–10 at varying dynamic levels.

LESSON 3

1. Play "Dry Bones" with the accompaniment track for your family and friends.

2. Practice Accent Dexterity Exercises #11–14 using bundle sticks or brushes.

UNIT 10

Creative Tools of Music

Allegretto—moderately quick tempo

Double Stops—two notes played simultaneously on a keyboard percussion insturment

Major—sequence of notes that defines the tonality of the major scale

Minor—a sequence of notes that defines the tonality of the minor scale

Minor Scale (natural)—a series of stepwise notes, up or down, with the ascending step pattern of whole, half, whole, whole, half, whole, whole

Pentatonic Scale—a five-note scale

Tonality—the relationship between notes and chords which establish a central pitch or harmony as the focal point

The Great Wave at Kanagawa, by Katsushika Hokusai

76 *Extension Warm-Up*

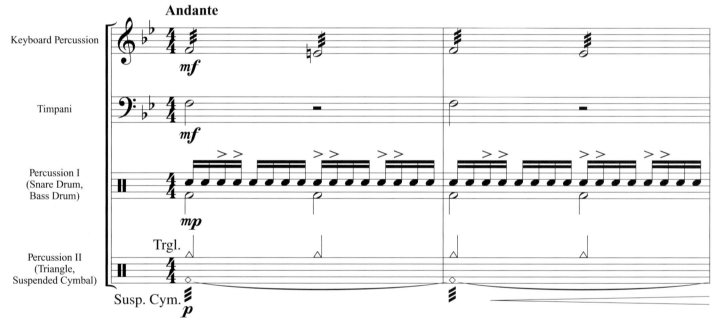

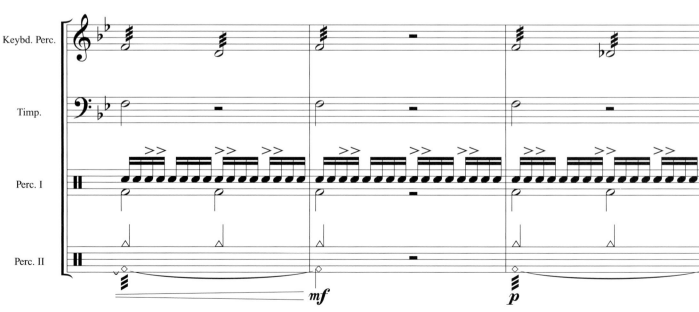

Line 76 continued

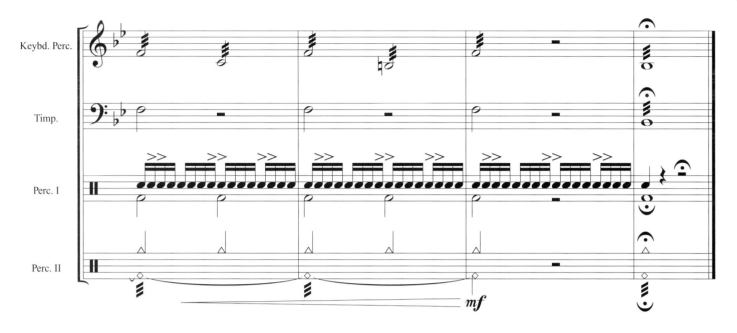

77 *New Note Chorale*

78 *The Willow Trees* CD : 27

Folk Song, Korea

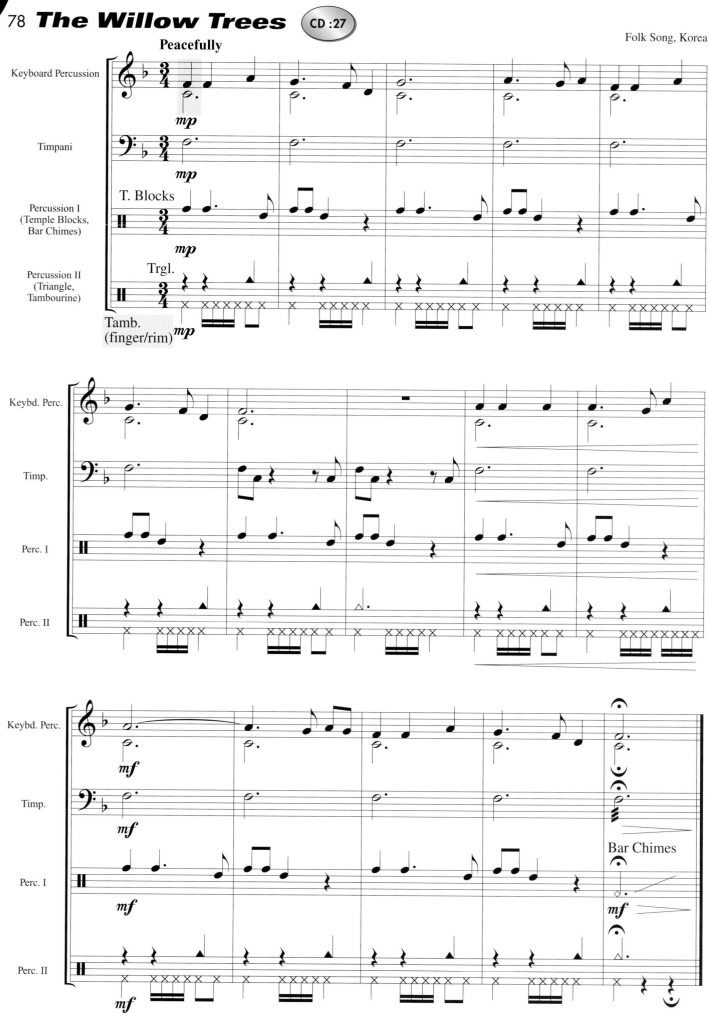

79 *Song of Kokkiriko*

Folk Song, Japan

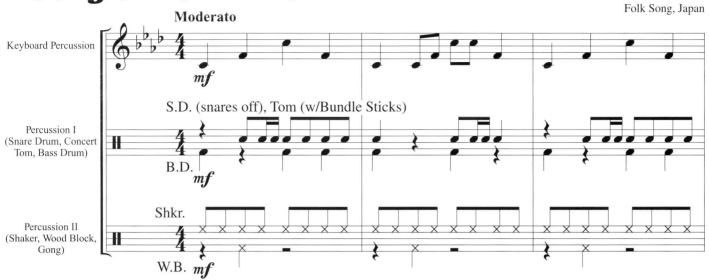

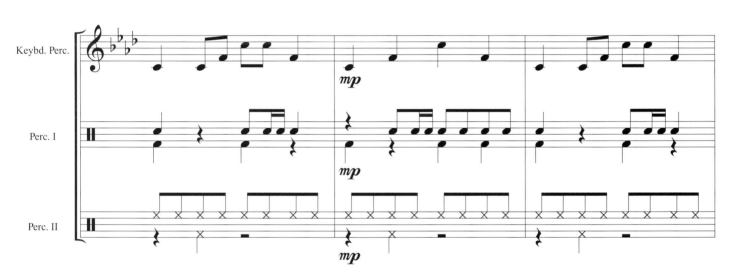

80 *Start and Release*

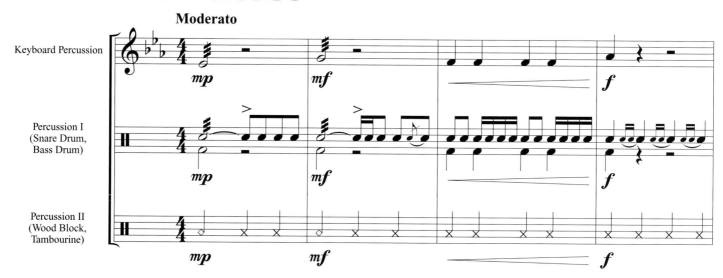

81 *Shalihonba* CD :28

Folk Song, China

Bouncy

Keyboard Percussion

Timpani

Percussion I
Four Drums,
(Four Toms,
Bongos/Timbales)

Percussion II
(Shaker,
Tambourine)

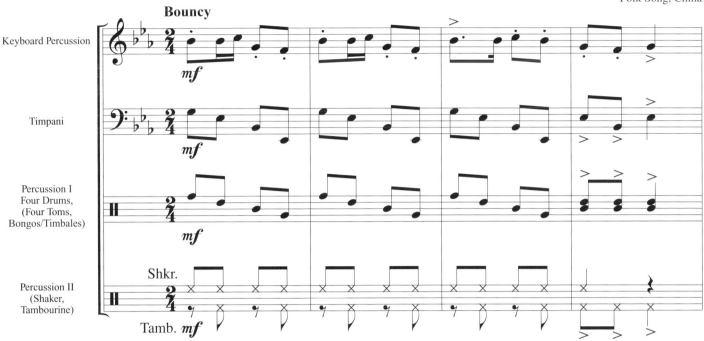

Keybd. Perc.

Timp.

Perc. I

Perc. II

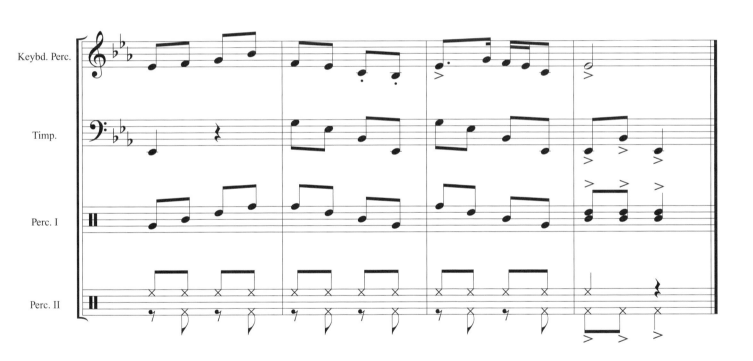

82 *Ode to Joy* (Major)

LUDWIG VAN BEETHOVEN, Germany

ine 82 continued

83 Ode to Joy (Minor)

CD :30

LUDWIG VAN BEETHOVEN, Germany

UNIT 10

Line 83 continued

84 *The Ship for the Kompira Shrine*

Folk Song, Japan

With strict rhythm

line 84 continued

(Play high E♭s if 32" Timp. is unavailable)

Band @ Home

LESSON 1

1. Practice the concert B♭ major scales on the "Treasury of Scales" page at 96 bpm.

2. Perform "The Willow Trees" with the accompaniment track for your family and friends.

3. Practice Accent Dexterity Exercises #15–16.

LESSON 2

1. Perform "Shalihonba" with the accompaniment track.

2. Practice Accent Dexterity Exercises #15–16.

LESSON 3

1. Compose a six-scale-degree pattern using the first five notes of the B♭ scale. We will perform this in our next class.

2. Play "The Ship for the Kompira Shrine" for your family and friends.

3. Practice Accent Dexterity Exercises #15–16 at different dynamic levels.

The Art of Playing Whistles

Rest Position

- The standard police whistle and siren whistle can be held in one hand.

Advanced Care and Maintenance

- Sanitize the lip plate by wiping it with mouthpiece disinfectant or mouthwash.

- Store the whistles in a separate bag and place in a designated area on a shelf or in the percussion cabinet drawer. Avoid placing other objects on top of the instrument.

Siren Whistle

- Hold the whistle away from your mouth to take in air prior to playing.

Slide Whistle

- Slide whistles require one hand to hold the whistle and the other hand to manipulate the plunger.

Police Whistle

- The characteristic sound of a whistle is a loud sustain created by blowing with a steady stream of air.

- Rhythms can be performed with small, quick bursts of air.

- Volume is produced by increasing the air speed. Less volume is produced by decreasing the air speed.

- Small whistles tend to produce very high tones and usually require a strong air stream to get the sound. Larger whistles produce lower tones and often will only sound with a gentle stream of air.

Creative Tools of Music

Arpeggio—the notes of a chord played in succession 1–3–5–8–5–3–1

Binary Form—form consisting of two parts: A and B

Form—the structure or framework of a composition

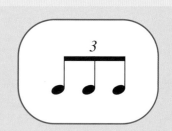

Wolfgang Amadeus Mozart

(b. Salzburg, January 27, 1756, d. Vienna, December 5, 1791) Wolfgang Amadeus Mozart is possibly the most famous composer from the classical period. His father Leopold, a prominent violinist and composer in Salzburg, began cultivating young Wolfgang's talent when his son was only three years old. By the time he was four Wolfgang was learning complex pieces on the piano by ear and performing them flawlessly after only one hour of practice. At the age of five he was already composing small pieces. Throughout his short life, Mozart composed hundreds of works, including symphonies, serenades, concertos, operas, choral pieces, chamber pieces, string quartets, piano quintets, and many pieces for keyboard. He died in poverty at the age of 35. Although under-appreciated during his lifetime, Mozart stands out as one of the most beloved and revered composers of all time.

Single Stroke Four

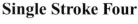
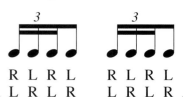

Single Stroke Seven

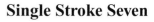

85 *Classical Chorale*

WOLFGANG AMADEUS MOZART, Austria

86 Themes from Eine Kleine Nachtmusik

WOLFGANG AMADEUS MOZART, Austria

UNIT 11
e 86 continued

87 *Pentascale Warm-Up*

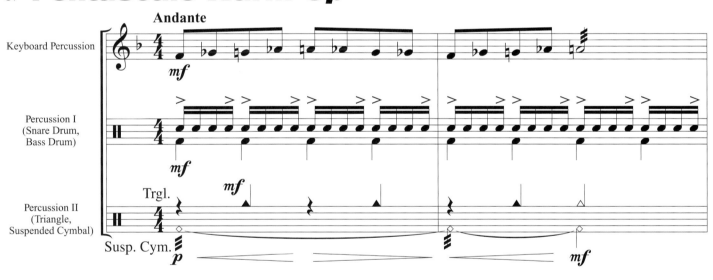

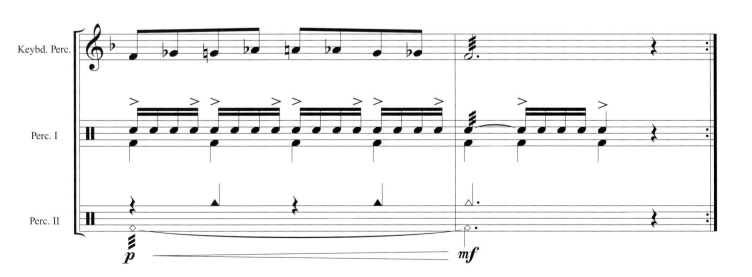

88 *Non Piu Andrai* CD :33
(From *The Marriage of Figaro*)

WOLFGANG AMADEUS MOZART, Austria

89 *Blueberry Pie*

90 ***Star Wars*** CD :34
(Main Theme)

Music by **JOHN WILLIAMS**

Majestic

91 *The Happy Whistler*

ROBERT SCHUMANN, Germany

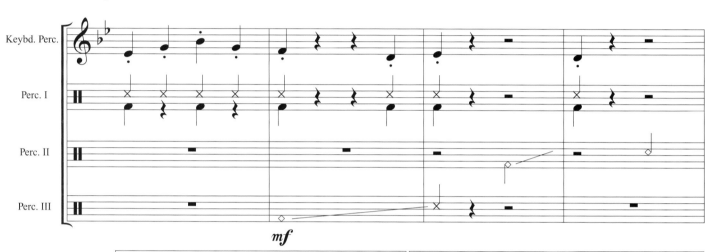

Band @ Home

LESSON 1

1. Perform "Themes from Eine Kleine Nachtmusik" for your family and friends. Be sure to inform them that Wolfgang Amadeus Mozart, a classical period composer, wrote it.

2. Practice Accent Dexterity Exercises #17–18.

LESSON 2

1. Create your own warm-up using the first five notes of the concert B♭ major scale. Be prepared to share it with the band in our next lesson.

2. Play "Non Piu Andrai" with the accompaniment track for your family and friends. Inform them that this is another composition by Wolfgang Amadeus Mozart.

3. Practice Accent Dexterity Exercises #17–18.

LESSON 3

1. Practice "Blueberry Pie" maintaining even eighth note triplets.

2. Practice "Star Wars (Main Theme)" with and without the accompaniment. Perform this piece for your family and friends.

3. Complete Worksheet #21: Writing Chords.

4. Practice the Single Stroke Four and Single Stroke Seven, "slow-fast-slow."

The Art of Playing Slapstick

Rest Position

- The slapstick (a sound effect also known as a whip) is available with or without a spring-hinge connecting two pieces of hardwood.

Ready Position

- Hold the slapstick at chest level with the boards spread apart.

Play Position

- Make a quick movement similar to clapping hands to make the sound of a cracking whip.

Advanced Care and Maintenance

- Place the slapstick in a designated area on a shelf or in the percussion cabinet drawer and avoid placing other objects on top of the instrument.

Creative Tools of Music

Ternary Form (ABA)—the form of a musical composition consisting of three sections

Cut Time (¢)—a symbol for the 2/2 time signature

New Notes: Concert G, F♯; See the position chart in the back of this book

Nine Lives, by Jim Tweedy

PORTRAIT

Clare Grundman

(1913–1996)

Clare Grundman was a very important 20th century American composer. He was born in New York in 1913, and went to school in Ohio before teaching arranging, woodwinds, and band at Ohio State University. Over a span of 50 years, he wrote more than 100 compositions and arrangements for bands. During World War II, he served as the Coast Guard's chief musician. After the war, he concentrated on composition and received many awards for his musical works for radio, television, motion pictures, ballet, and Broadway musical productions. Many of Grundman's band arrangements were based on folk song melodies. These include works such as "American Folk Rhapsody No. 3," "An Irish Rhapsody," "Concord," and "Fantasy on American Sailing Songs." He also arranged works by noted composers Leonard Bernstein, Aaron Copland, Gustav Holst, and Edward Elgar. Clare Grundman died in 1996.

Cut Time

¢ = **2/2** = beats in a measure
= half note/rest receives one beat

92 Concert G Minor Scale

93 Canoe Song CD :35

Camp Song, U.S.A.

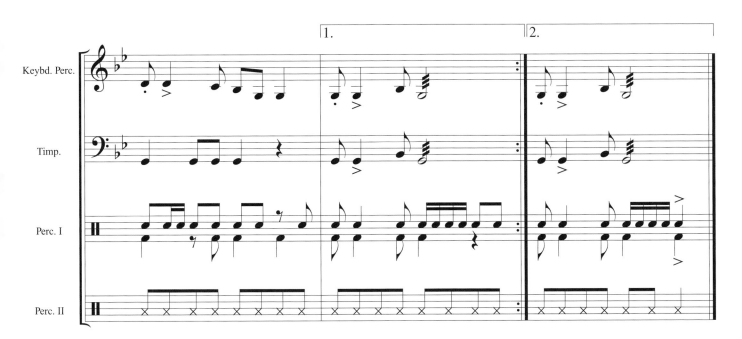

UNIT 12

94 *Finale from the "New World Symphony"*

ANTONÍN DVOŘÁK, Czech Republic

95 *Coventry Chorale*

Traditional Melody, England

Butter Fingers

96 *Songs of the Sea*

Traditional Sea Chanties

ine 96 continued

97 *Dynamic Changes*

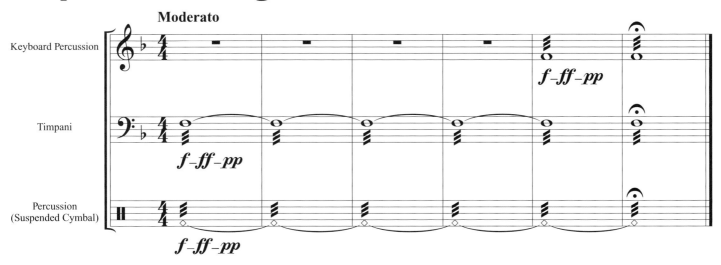

98 *"Trio" from "The Stars and Stripes Forever"*

JOHN PHILIP SOUSA, U.S.A.

March style

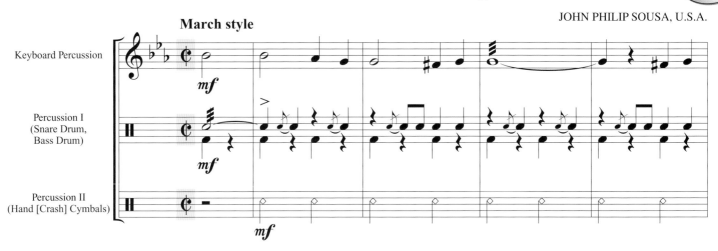

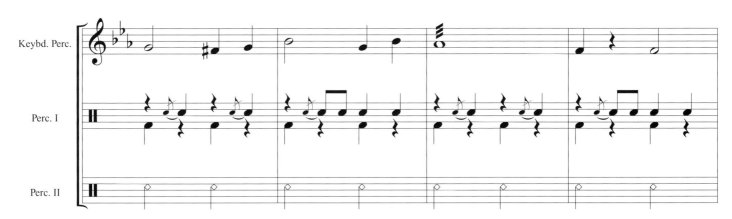

me 98 continued

UNIT 12

Ready Position

Play Position

99 ***Merrily We Roll Along*** CD :38

Words and Music by
EDDIE CANTOR, CHARLIE TOBIAS
and MURRAY MENCHER

ine 99 continued

Band @ Home

LESSON 1

1. Perform "Canoe Song" with the accompaniment track for your family and friends.

2. Practice "Concert G Minor Scale" in whole notes and then in half and quarter note rhythmic combinations.

3. Practice Accent Dexterity Exercises #19–20.

LESSON 2

1. Practice the concert G minor scale.

2. Practice "Songs of the Sea" and explain ABA form to a family member.

3. Practice Accent Dexterity Exercises #19–20.

LESSON 3

1. Practice and perform the "Trio" From "The Stars and Stripes Forever" with the accompaniment track for your family and friends.

2. Perform "Merrily We Roll Along" with the accompaniment track for your family and friends.

3. Practice Accent Dexterity Exercises #19–20.

Creative Tools of Music

Climax—the point at which music arrives at its most exciting moment

Cue—in conducting, a gesture to signal an entrance; or, small notes to play as an option

Fanfare—a short, lively, and loud composition usually with brass and timpani

Key Change—changing from one key to another key within a musical composition

Macro—a prefix meaning large, inclusive

Maestoso—majestic or stately

Marcato(ᴧ)—a style of playing notes emphasized and slightly separated

Rit. (Ritardando)—gradually slower

Shape and Contour—the direction of a melody through dynamics, pitch levels, and rhythm

Soli—a line of music played by a small group of instruments

Tacet—do not play

Tutti—all play

Sticking System

Creating a sticking system (assigning a specific hand to play a rhythm) for the snare drum is necessary to develop proper muscle memory that will aid the student in creating a consistent approach to reading and performing rhythms. The "right-hand-lead" system is a sticking system that promotes a uniform approach to playing repeated rhythms, develops a more consistent quality of sound, improves ensemble precision, and enhances the ability to sight-read.

Develop a sticking pattern from the smallest subdivision of the beat in a measure. Base the sticking for rhythm figures in simple and compound time on natural alternating strokes. Groups of "after beat" rhythms and "steady pulse" rhythms can be performed by using either the right-hand-lead system or an alternated sticking.

Sixteenth note rhythms

Eighth note rhythms

Quarter note rhythms

Compound and triplet rhythms

100 *Concert F Chromatic Warm-Up*

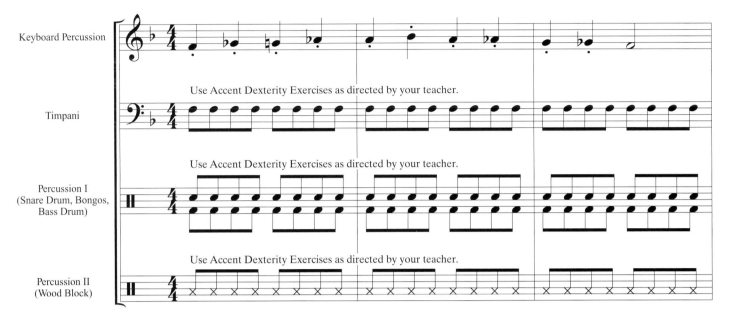

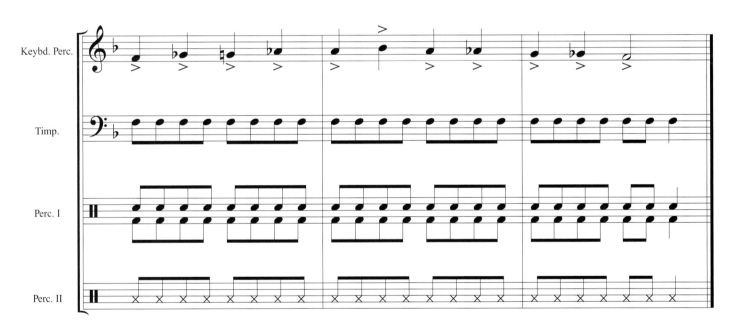

101 *Revenge of the Slurs—Tacet*

102 *Fanfare for the Season*
"Joy to the World" and "Hark! The Herald Angels Sing"

CD :39

"Joy to the World"
by LOWELL MASON, U.S.A.
"Hark! The Herald Angels Sing"
by FELIX MENDELSSOHN, Germany
Arranged by ROBERT W. SMITH

ne 102 continued

e prepared for you or your standmate to quickly turn the page.

Line 102 continued

To Snare/Bass Drums

36 Maestoso

ne 102 continued

103 *Greensleeves*   CD :40

Traditional, England
Arranged by ROBERT W. SMITH (ASCAP)

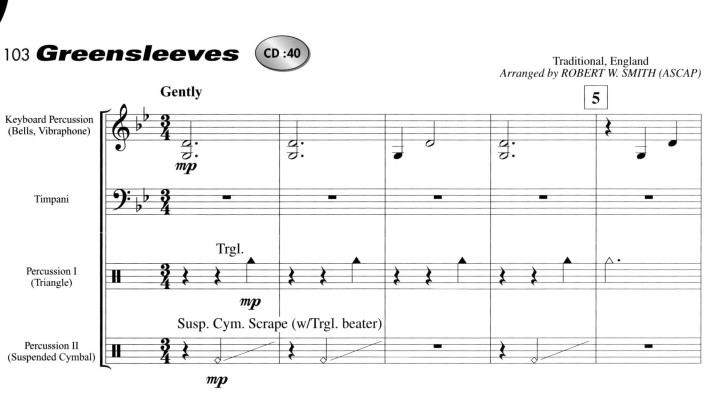

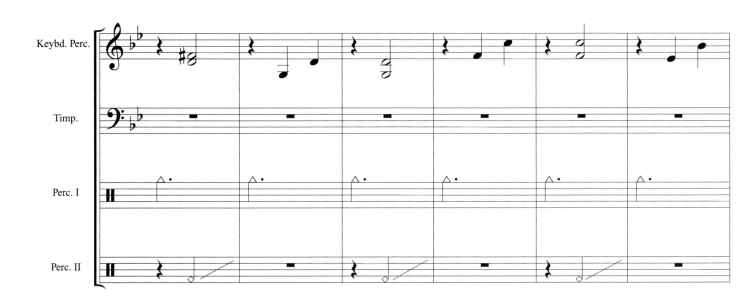

ne 103 continued

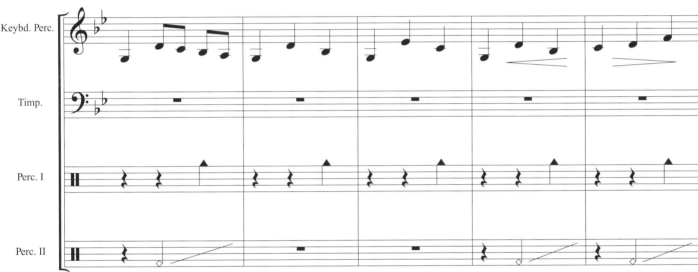

29

e prepared for you or your standmate to quickly turn the page.

Line 103 continued

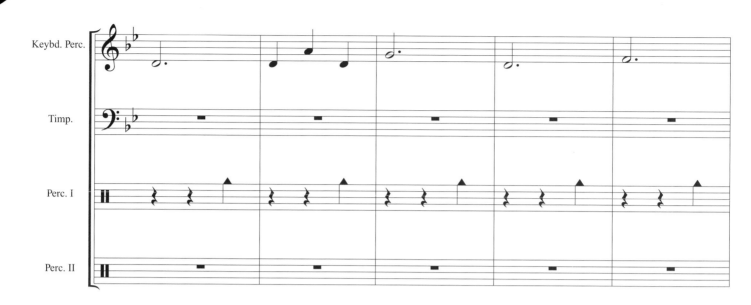

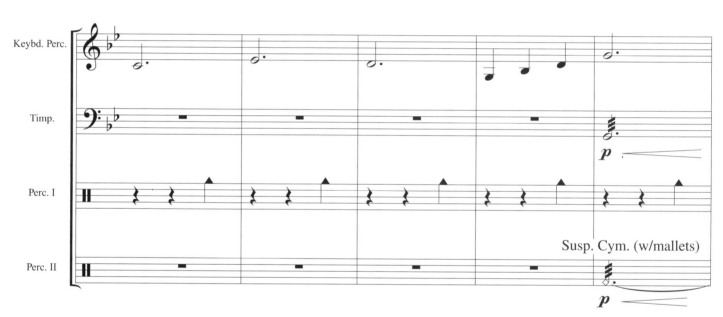

45 **Flowing**

ine 103 continued

61

Scrape (w/Trgl. beater)

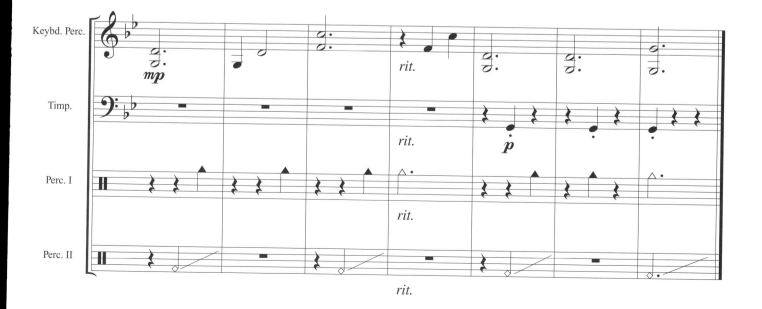

104 **Coventry Chorale** CD :41

Traditional, England

105 **Festival of Lights**
A Hanukkah Celebration

CD :42

"Mr. Shamash" Traditional Hanukkah Song
"Dreidle Song" Traditional Hanukkah Song
Arranged by ROBERT W. SMITH

Be prepared for you or your standmate to quickly turn the page.

Line 105 continued

Line 105 continued

106 Sleigh Ride CD :43

Music by LEROY ANDERSON
Arranged by MICHAEL STORY

Ine 106 continued

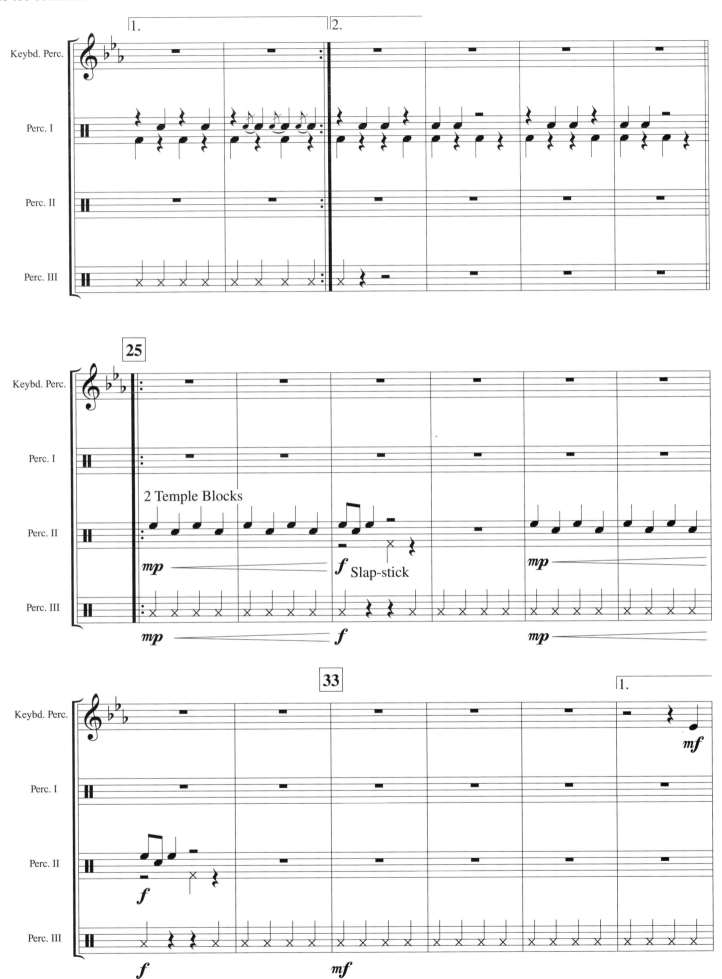

Be prepared for you or your standmate to quickly turn the page.

Line 106 continued

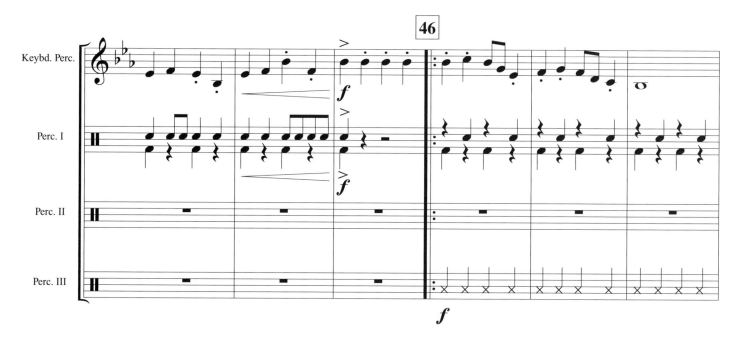

ne 106 continued

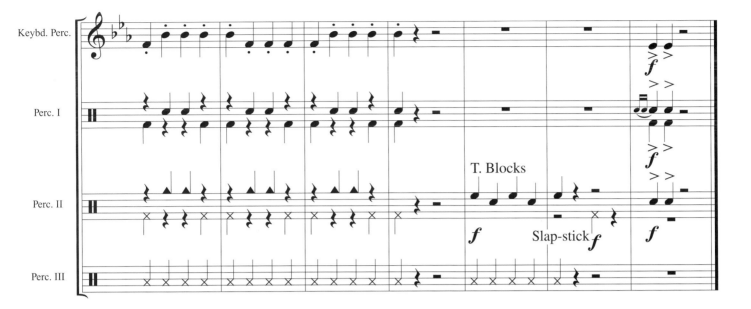

Solos:

Log on to www.band-expressions.com to download the music for these solos.

07 *A New Year! (Auld Lang Syne)* CD :44

08 *Winter Wonderland* CD :45

UNITS 16–18 WILL BE PRESENTED BY YOUR TEACHER

UNIT 19

Creative Tools of Music

Overture—a single musical work that introduces an opera, play, ballet, or longer musical work

- **Triangle:** Close the fingers of the holding hand around the top corner of the triangle for a closed sound. Remove the fingers to allow the triangle to ring freely.

- **Cowbell:** Use the tip of the index finger to dampen the cowbell to achieve a closed sound. Remove the finger to allow the cowbell to ring freely.

- **Hi-hat:** Use the foot to control the open and closed sound of the hi-hat cymbals.

- **Suspended Cymbal:** Dampen the suspended cymbal next to the strike area with a free hand to achieve a closed sound. Remove the hand to allow the cymbal to ring freely.

109 *Concert B♭ Chromatic Warm-Up*

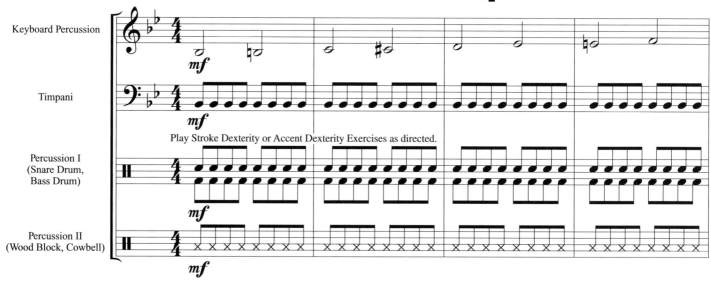

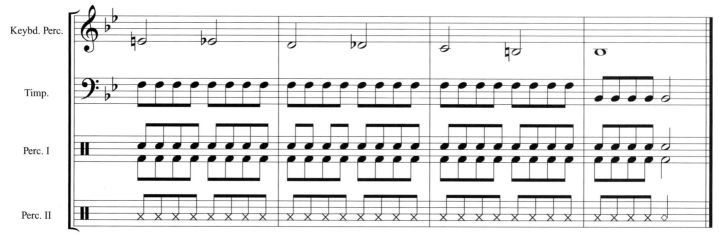

ÍNDICE

UNIT 19

reative Tools of Music

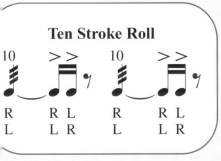

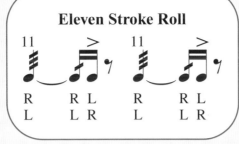

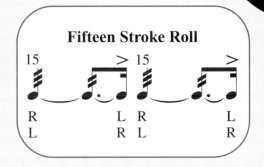

110 **Chromatic Chorale** CD :46

111 *Concert B♭ Chromatic Scale*

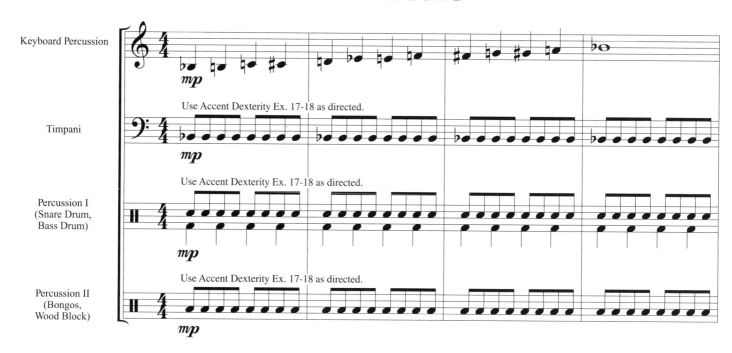

UNIT 19

112 **Brookshire Melody**

UNIT 19

113 *Flight of the Bumblebee*

NIKOLAI RIMSKY-KORSAKOV, Russia

ne 113 continued

UNIT 19

114 *Arborhill March*

115 *Scale Focus Warm-Up*

116 Town Lake Samba

CD :49

(Take 2nd ending on the D.C.)

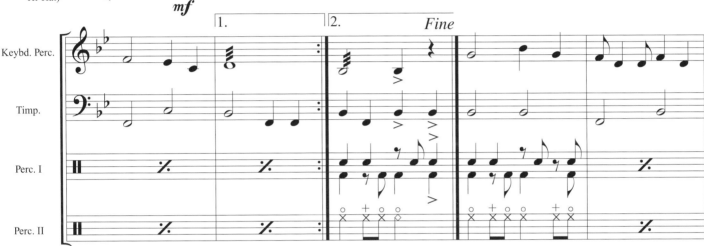

Band @ Home

LESSON 1

1. Practice and memorize the concert Bb chromatic scale. Gradually increase the tempo. Be sure to keep the pulse steady and the notes even.

2. Perform "Chromatic Chorale" with the accompaniment track.

3. Review Accent Dexterity Exercises #11–20.

LESSON 2

1. Practice the concert Bb chromatic scale from memory, gradually increasing the tempo.

2. Perform" Flight of the Bumblebee" with the accompaniment track.

3. Practice improvising a two measure chromatic melody using any of the notes in your chromatic scale in 4/4 meter with and without the accompaniment track. Some students may play this improvisation for the class at our next meeting.

CD :48

4. Practice the 10-, 11-, and 15-Stroke Rolls from slow to fast to slow. Practice the new rolls as both multiple bounce and double stroke rolls.

LESSON 3

1. Continue to practice your concert Bb chromatic scale from memory, gradually increasing the tempo. Rhythmically improvise on the scale.

2. Perform "Town Lake Samba" with the accompaniment track.

3. Continue to practice the 10-, 11-, and 15-Stroke Rolls from slow to fast to slow. Remember to practice all rolls as both multiple bounce and double stroke rolls.

UNIT 20

The Art of Playing Kick Drum

Setup Procedure

- Stand behind the kick drum with your feet comfortably spread apart.

- Sitting on a stool will help the taller player to better position the leg properly and to work the pedal more efficiently.

Ready Position

- Place your right foot flat on the bass drum pedal. Stay relaxed so that the beater remains off the head.

Play Position

- Make a quick downward stroke with your toe to sound the kick drum. Relax the foot to allow the beater to naturally spring from the head.

- Keep the entire foot relaxed and in contact with the pedal throughout the stroke

117A *Chromatic in Eighths*

117B *Chromatic in Eighths*

Creative Tools of Music

4/8 = beats in a measure = eighth note/rest receives one beat

6/8 = beats in a measure = eighth note/rest receives one beat

3/8 = beats in a measure = eighth note/rest receives one beat

African Village

ne 117B continued

117C *Chromatic in Eighths*

118 The Hey Song CD :50

Words and Music by
MIKE LEANDER
and GARY GLITTER

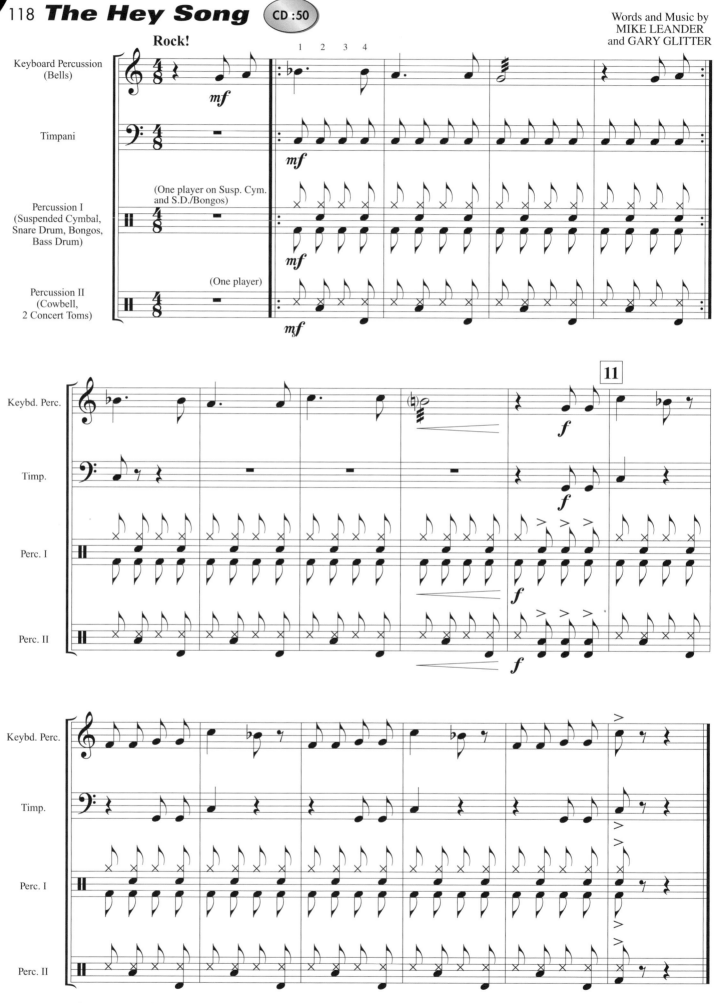

119 **_Allunde, Alluia_** CD :51

Swahili Lullaby, Africa

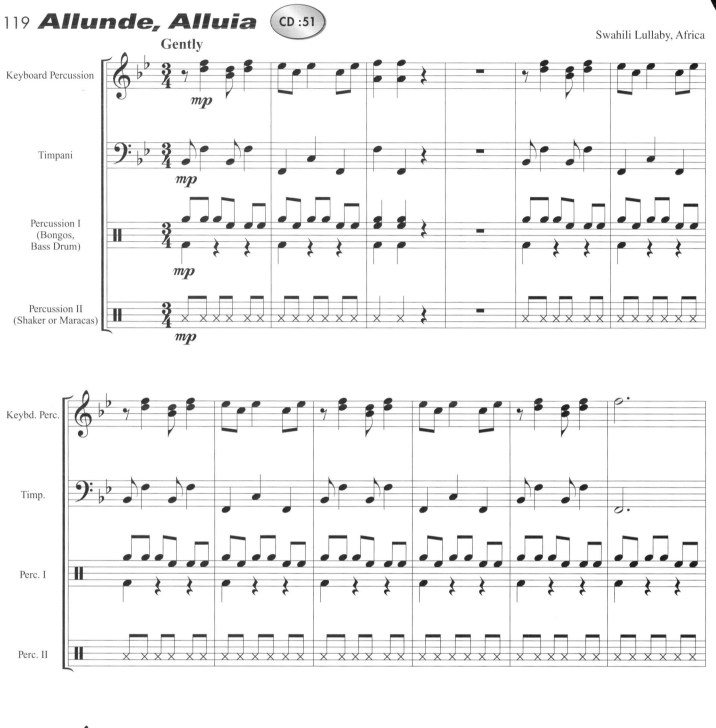

UNIT 20

120 Windsor Hills Chorale

121 The Lion Sleeps Tonight CD :52

Words and Music by
GEORGE DAVID WEISS, HUGO PERETTI
and LUIGI CREATORE

Ine 121 continued

122 *African Echoes*

Moderately fast

122P *African Echoes*

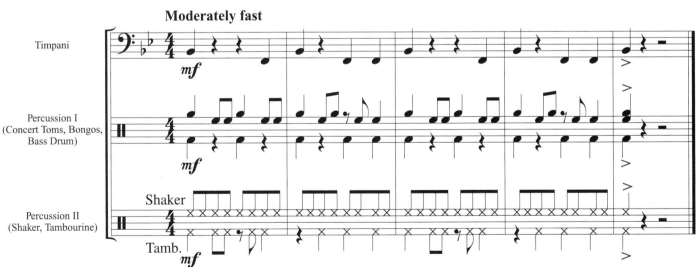

123 *Two African Songs*

T'hola T'hola and *Everybody Loves Saturday Night*

T'hola T'hola, South Africa
Everybody Loves Saturday Night, Nigeria

UNIT 20

ine 123 continued

Band @ Home

LESSON 1

1. Continue to practice the concert B♭ chromatic scale from memory, gradually increasing the tempo.

2. Perform "The Hey Song" with the accompaniment track.

3. Continue to practice the 10-, 11-, and 15-Stroke Rolls from slow to fast to slow and learn Accent Dexterity Exercises #21–22.

LESSON 2

1. Using Worksheet #42, compose a four-measure phrase in 6/8 in the key of Concert F. Be prepared to play your composition.

2. Continue to increase the speed of the concert B♭ chromatic scale. Practice the scale using different time signatures that you have learned.

3. Continue to practice the 10-, 11-, and 15-Stroke Rolls from slow to fast to slow and review Accent Dexterity Exercises #23–24.

LESSON 3

1. Perform your composition for your family using the CD accompaniment.

2. Perform "The Lion Sleeps Tonight" with the CD accompaniment for your family.

3. Practice Accent Dexterity Exercises #21–24.

155

Creative Tools of Music

Review

Accelerando—gradually faster

Simple Meter—meter in which each beat in a measure can be divided by two (2/4, 3/4, 4/4)

Compound Meter—meter in which each beat in a measure can be divided by three (6/8, 9/8, 12/8)

Subdivide—break down a beat into smaller divisions

Tertian—a harmonic system based on the interval of a third

Two Over Three, by Tom Berg

PORTRAIT

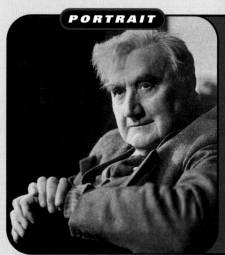

Ralph Vaughan Williams

Ralph (pronounced "Rafe") Vaughan Williams was born in Gloucestershire, England in 1872, and is considered by many as the greatest British composer of the twentieth century. Vaughan Williams composed music for most types of instrumental and vocal ensembles. His original pieces and arrangements of British folksongs and hymn tunes are some of the most popular in the English language. Some of Williams' works include *A Sea Symphony; Fantasia on a Theme*, his first masterwork; the opera, *The Pilgrim's Progress;* his first orchestral symphony, *A London Symphony;* and the pastoral, *The Lark Ascending* for violin and orchestra. In addition, he is considered on of the most prolific contributors to church music in the twentieth century. In a long and productive life, the music that flowed from his creative pen included nine symphonies, five operas, film music, ballet and stage music, several song cycles, church music, and works for chorus and orchestra. In 1935, he received the Order of Merit, an honor bestowed by the Queen of England upon those few that have rendered exceptionally meritorious service towards the advancement of the Arts, Learning, Literature, and Science. A champion of British cultural heritage in is own unique way, he died at the age of 85 in 1958, and his ashes are fittingly interred in Westminster Abbey.

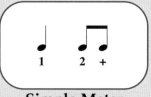

Simple Meter

Compound Meter

Flam Accent

124 *Tertian Chorale*

125 *Extreme Velocity*

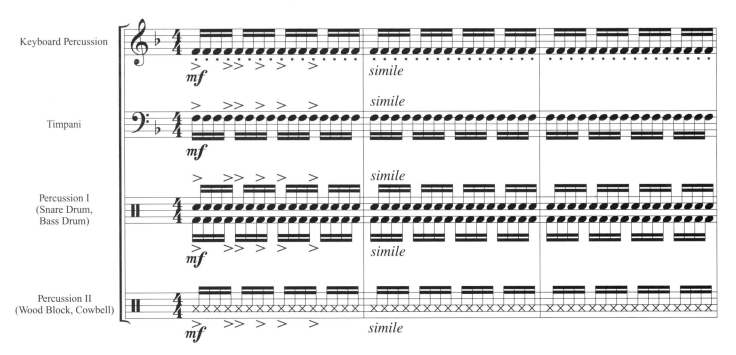

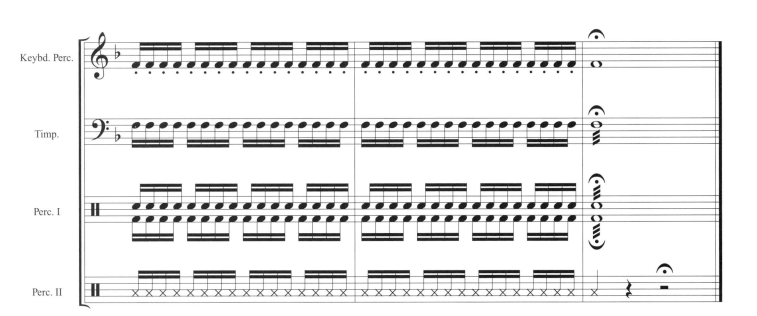

UNIT 21

126 **Sabre Dance**

ARAM IL'YICH KHACHATURIAN, Armenia/Russia

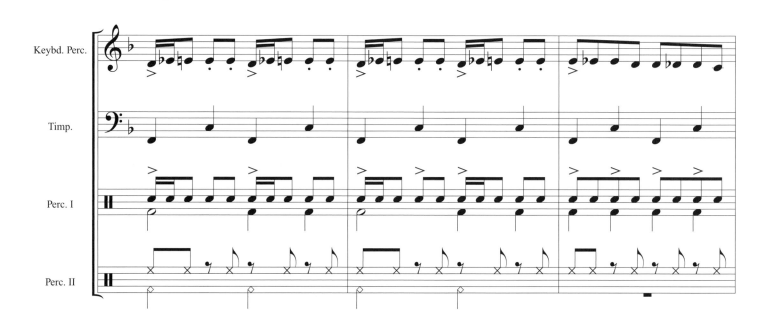

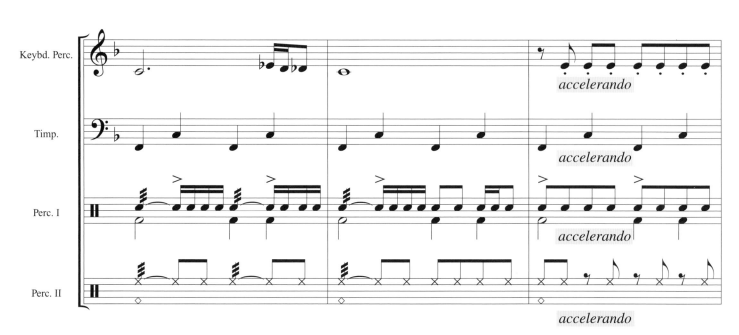

UNIT 21

127 *Fanfare* CD :55

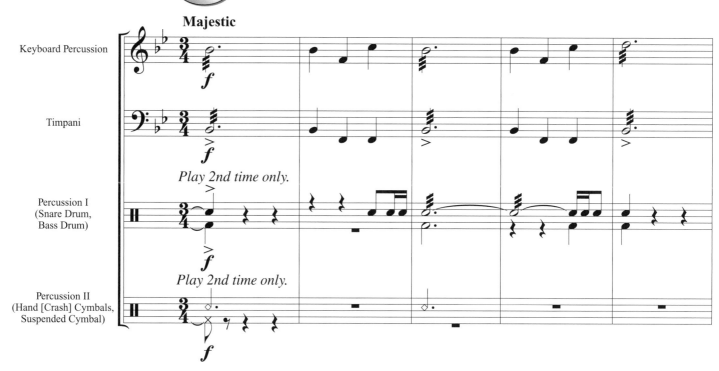

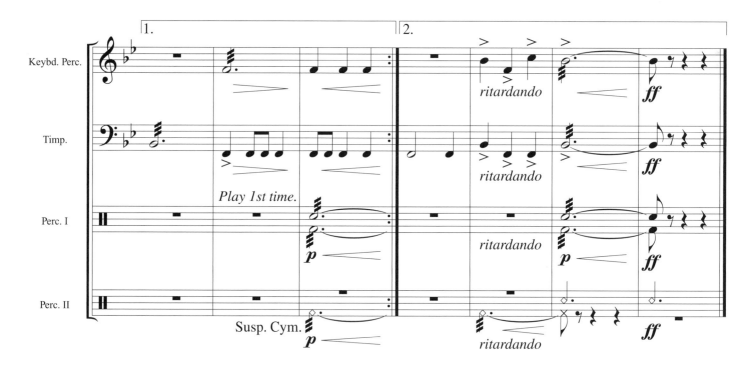

128 ***Morris Dance (Simple Meter)***

Folk Song, England

129 Morris Dance (Compound Meter)

Folk Song, England

130 *Mixing the Eighths*

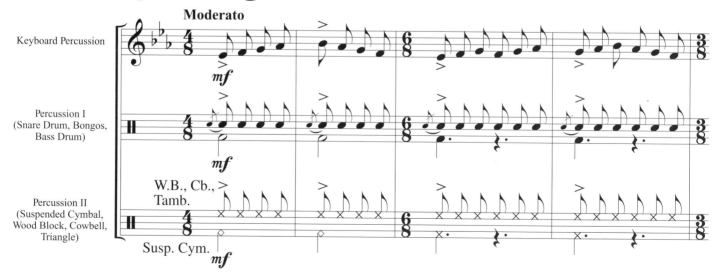

ne 130 continued

Band @ Home

LESSON 1

1. Warm up with "Tertian Chorale." Be sure to play and sing each of the parts in preparation for the next class.

2. Practice "Extreme Velocity" beginning at 98 bpm. Gradually increase the tempo with each repetition. What is the fastest tempo you can play "Extreme Velocity?"

3. Practice "Sabre Dance" with the accompaniment track. After you are comfortable with your performance, play "Sabre Dance" for your family and friends. Be sure to inform them that it is a dance made famous by Russian composer Aram Khatchaturian.

4. Continue practicing Accent Dexterity Exercises #25–28, increasing the tempo as you gain proficiency.

LESSON 2

1. Practice "Extreme Velocity" beginning at 98 bpm. Gradually increase the tempo with each repetition.

2. Practice "Morris Dance" in both simple and compound meter.

3. Continue practicing Accent Dexterity Exercises #25–28 increasing in tempo as you gain proficiency.

LESSON 3

1. Practice "Extreme Velocity" beginning at 98 bpm. Gradually increase the tempo with each repetition.

2. Practice "Morris Dance" in both simple and compound meter.

3. Perform "Fanfare" with the accompaniment track for your family and friends.

4. Continue practicing Accent Dexterity Exercises #25–28, increasing the tempo as you gain proficiency.

UNIT 22

Creative Tools of Music

a tempo—return to the previous tempo

D.C. al Coda—return to the beginning and play the Coda ending

Fortepiano(_fp_)—play loud and then immediately play soft

Harmonic Minor Scale—the same as the natural minor scale, except that the seventh tone is raised by a half step both ascending and descending

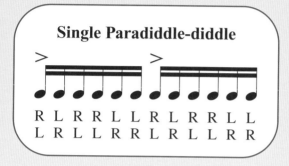

$\frac{9}{8}$ = nine/three beats in a measure

= eighth/dotted quarter note/rest receives one be...

$\frac{12}{8}$ = twelve/four beats in a measure

= eighth/dotted quarter note/rest receives one be...

Single Paradiddle-diddle

R L R R L L R L R R L L
L R L L R R L R L L R R

131 *A Tempo Chorale*

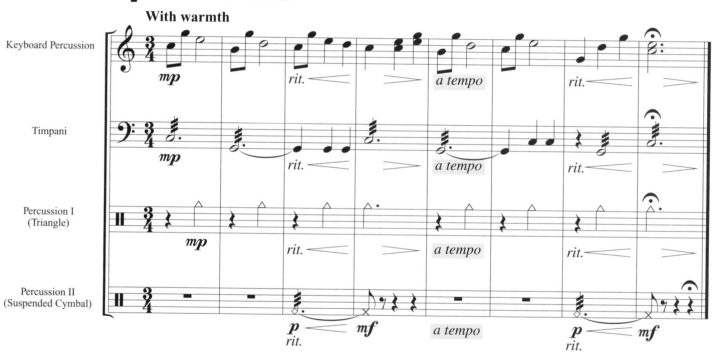

With warmth

Keyboard Percussion

Timpani

Percussion I (Triangle)

Percussion II (Suspended Cymbal)

132 ***We're Off to See the Wizard***

Music by HAROLD ARLEN
Lyrics by E.Y. HARBURG

133 *Irish Washerwoman*

Traditional, Ireland

134 Jesu, Joy of Man's Desiring

JOHANN SEBASTIAN BACH, Germany

135 Concert C Harmonic Minor Scale

136 **Sing, Sing, Sing**   CD :57

Words and Music by LOUIS PRIMA, U.S.A.

Swish Position

- The swish technique creates a soft, sustained shimmer when the edge of one cymbal scrapes the grooves of another.

- Hold the left cymbal stationary at chest level.

- Place the edge of the right cymbal just above the inside bell area of the left cymbal.

- Slide the edge of the right cymbal upward in a smooth quick motion as you scrape the grooves.

- Start the scrape motion just before the written note of the swish so that it finishes on the beat.

137 *Greensleeves*

Traditional, England

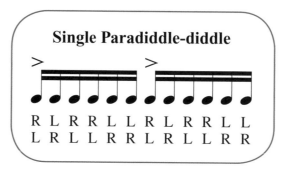

Single Paradiddle-diddle

138 *When Johnny Comes Marching Home*

Traditional, U.S.A.

ne 138 continued

Band @ Home

1. Warm up with "A tempo Chorale."

2. Practice "Irish Washerwoman" beginning at a slow tempo. Gradually increase the tempo with each repetition. What is the fastest tempo you can play "Irish Washerwoman?"

3. Practice "We're Off to See the Wizard." After you are comfortable with your performance, play "We're Off to See the Wizard" for your family and friends. Be sure to inform them that it is a song from "The Wizard of Oz."

4. Continue practicing Accent Dexterity Exercises #29–30, increasing the tempo as you gain proficiency.

1. Practice "Jesu, Joy of Man's Desiring."

2. Practice "Sing, Sing, Sing" with the accompaniment track.

3. Continue practicing Accent Dexterity Exercise #31, increasing the tempo as you gain proficiency.

1. Warm up playing "Greensleeves."

2. Practice "When Johnny Comes Marching Home" with the accompaniment track.

3. Practice the Paradiddle-diddle, starting with either hand, and Accent Dexterity Exercises 29–32 at a variety of dynamic levels.

Creative Tools of Music

Ragtime—an early form of jazz that reached its peak c. 1910-1915

Trill (*tr*)—a musical symbol or term meaning to alternate rapidly between two adjacent pitches.

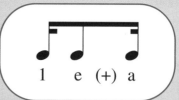

1   e   (+)   a

PORTRAIT

Scott Joplin
1867(?)-1917

Scott Joplin was a famous African-American composer. His pieces employed the technique of "ragging the scale." This described the syncopation in his music. The style of music that Joplin perfected was called "ragtime." Individual pieces of music are called "rags."

Scott Joplin's exact date of birth is not known, but it is believed that he was born between mid-1867 and early 1868. Joplin's musical talent was recognized early in his life. In August of 1899, he published his famous "Maple Leaf Rag." This has become one of the greatest and most famous of all piano rags. Three years later he composed "The Entertainer," another very famous piano rag.

Joplin's music was used in the 1973 film, "The Sting." In 1976, the Pulitzer Committee issued an award to Scott Joplin for his contribution to American music.

Vampin' (Piney Brown Blues), by Romare Bearde

139 *Ragtime Sixteenths* CD :59

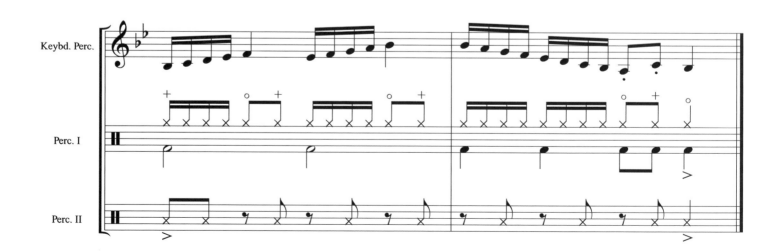

140 *The Entertainer* CD :60

SCOTT JOPLIN, U.S.A.

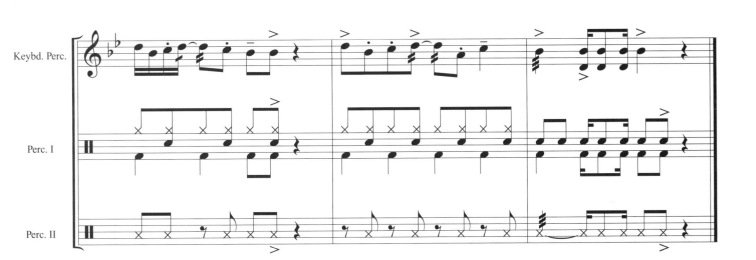

141 *Maple Leaf Rag*

SCOTT JOPLIN, U.S.A.

Ragtime

142 *Li'l Liza Jane* CD :61

Words and Music by
COUNTESS ADA DELACHAU, U.S.A.

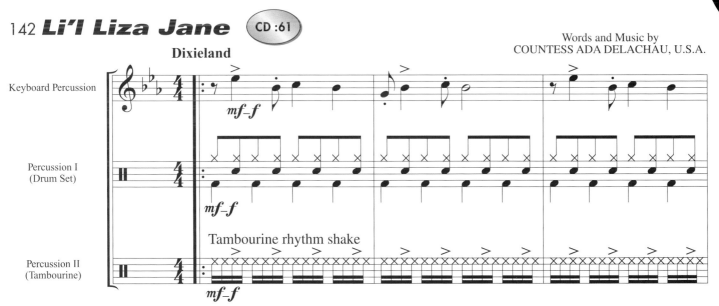

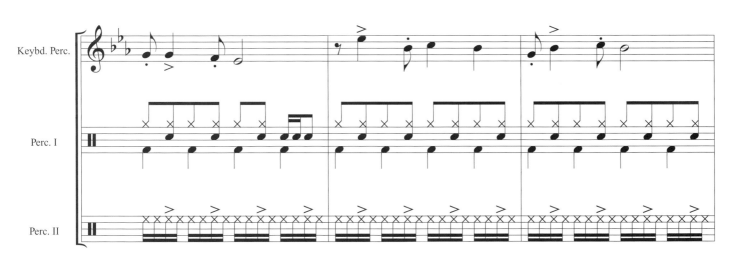

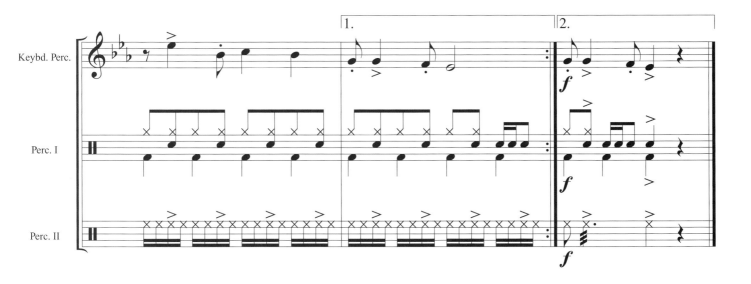

143 *When the Saints Go Marching In* CD :62

Words and Music by
JAMES M. BLACK and
KATHERINE E. PURVIS, U.S.A.

144 *Just for the Trill of It*

Band @ Home

LESSON 1

1. Practice singing a concert F and check by playing the note on your instrument to see how accurate you were.

2. Play various scales from the "Treasury of Scales" portion of your book. Try to play longer each day to build endurance.

3. Practice "The Entertainer" and then perform with the accompaniment track for your family and friends.

4. Practice Accent Dexterity Exercise #33.

LESSON 2

1. Practice singing a concert F and check by playing the note on your instrument to see how close you came.

2. Play various scales from the "Treasury of Scales" portion of your book. Try to make your practice session longer each day to build endurance.

3. Improvise a two-measure melody with the sixteenth-eighth-sixteenth rhythm pattern.

4. Practice and perform "Maple Leaf Rag." Explain what you know about the composer, Scott Joplin, to your family and friends.

5. Practice Accent Dexterity Exercise #34.

LESSON 3

1. Practice singing a concert F and check by playing the note on your instrument to see how close you came.

2. Play various scales from the "Treasury of Scales" portion of your book. Try to play longer each day to build endurance.

3. Practice "Li'L Liza Jane" and "When the Saints Go Marching In."

4. Practice trilling on various pitches. Practice "Just for the Trill of It."

5. Practice Accent Dexterity Exercise #34 and air drum "Li'l Liza Jane" to practice your three-way coordination.

Creative Tools of Music

Review

Molto—very or much

Texture—the vertical elements of music,
including melodies, harmonies, rhythms,
and instruments

New Note: Concert D;
See the position chart in
the back of this book

Tempo	Metronome Marking	Definition
Allegro	120–168	Fast tempo
Allegretto	110–132	Quick tempo
Moderato	108–120	Moderate or medium tempo
Andante	76–107	Moderately Slow (walking) tempo
Lento	58–76	Slow tempo
Largo	40–58	Very Slow Tempo

PORTRAIT

Peter Ilyich Tchaikovsky

Peter Ilyich Tchaikovsky was born May 7, 1840, in northern Russia. He is recognized as one of the leading composers of the Romantic period. Tchaikovsky earned a degree as a lawyer but realized that his real interest lay in music. He taught harmony at the Moscow Conservatory and soon plunged into composition. One of his first successes was the ballet *Romeo and Juliet*. Tchaikovsky composed operas, but he is most famous for his symphonies, piano and string concertos, and ballet music, including *Swan Lake, The Sleeping Beauty,* and *The Nutcracker.* One of the most famous pieces in symphonic literature is Tchaikovsky's *1812 Overture.* Much of his music was influenced by his Russian heritage, and his greatest works were completed in the last six years of his life. He died November 6, 1893, at age 53.

Swiss Army Triplet

145 *Chorale*
(From *1812 Overture*)

PETER ILYICH TCHAIKOVSKY, Russia

146 Morning Mood

(From *Peer Gynt Suite*)

EDVARD GRIEG, Norway

147 *March Nationale*

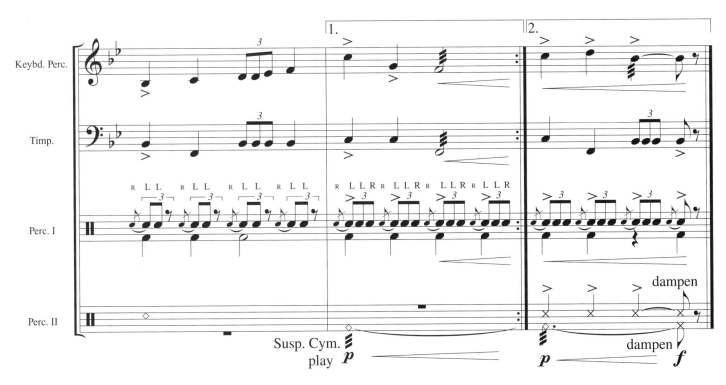

148 Sleeping Beauty CD :63

PETER ILYICH TCHAIKOVSKY, Russia

149 *Die Meistersinger*

RICHARD WAGNER, Germany

UNIT 24

150 *Brahms Lullaby*

JOHANNES BRAHMS, Germany

Gently, yet expressive

151 *March of the Toy Soldiers* CD :64

PETER ILYICH TCHAIKOVSKY, Russia

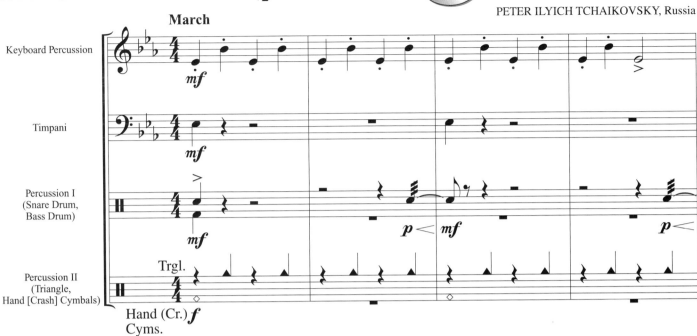

Band @ Home

LESSON 1

1. Practice singing a concert F and check by playing the note on your instrument to see how accurate you were.

2. Practice "Morning Mood" and "March Nationale," and then perform for your family and friends.

3. Practice the Swiss Army Triplet.

LESSON 2

1. Practice "Sleeping Beauty" and then perform for your family and friends with the accompaniment track. Inform them of what you know about the composer, Peter Ilyich Tchaikovsky.

2. Practice Accent Dexterity Exercise #35.

3. Complete Worksheet #51: I, IV, and V Chord.

LESSON 3

1. Listen to and identify the three types of texture.

2. Which type of texture would you choose to accompany your composition on Worksheet #51?

3. Practice "March of the Toy Soldiers." Perform it with the accompaniment track.

4. Practice Accent Dexterity Exercise #36.

Monophony: CD :65

Polyphony: CD :66

Homophony: CD :67

The Art of Playing Drumset

History

1. The drum set, also known as a drum kit, is a collection of percussion instruments set up around a stool (throne), so that a single percussionist can sit while playing several instruments at once. Typical instruments in a modern drum set include a snare drum; a small bass drum called a kick drum that is struck with a foot pedal; hi-hat, crash, and ride cymbals; one or two mid-range tom-toms, and a low-range floor tom-tom.

2. The drum set originated in early twentieth-century Dixieland music as two or more marching drummers moved inside to perform music for dances and other social events. The invention of foot-controlled bass drum pedals and hi-hat cymbals added flexibility as one drummer assumed the responsibilities for playing the growing collection of drums and cymbals.

Advanced Care and Maintenance

- Use a cloth to keep the entire drum set clean and free of fingerprints, dust, and dirt.

- The average life of a plastic drum head is one year. Replace worn or damaged heads immediately.

- Keep all objects off of the drum set; it's not a table.

- A small dab of lithium grease or lug lubrication should be occasionally applied to the tension rods to aid in tuning.

Tuning

- The snare drum serves as one of the focus instruments of the drum set and can be tuned similarly to a concert snare drum.

- The kick drum (inside) batter head can be tuned medium-low to provide good response from the bass drum pedal. Tune the (outside) resonating head slightly higher for added resonance. Internal muffling may be added to limit the resonance.

- Tune both the batter head and the resonating head of each tom-tom to th same medium pitch to produce a clear resonant sound. Tighter heads produce a bright, dry tone and looser heads produce a deep, "fat" tone.

- The tom-toms should be tuned at least the interval of a third apart in pitch. Wider intervals will create even more contrast when the drums are played sequentially.

Rest Position

- The drums should be set-up around you with each individual instrumen placed at a position that provides a comfortable reach.

- The use of a height-adjustable stool (throne) is necessary to allow each individual the opportunity to play in a position that provides comfortabl access to the foot pedals.

- Each individual student should experiment with drum and cymbal setup as well as throne height and location to find the position that allows for the greatest freedom of movement and ease of playing.

Ready Position

- Use the same ready position as that for the concert snare drum.

Play Position

- Use a full stroke to play on any surface on the drum set. Limit the angle and distance each stroke must make so that the stick motion is smooth and relaxed.

Multiple Mallet Grip

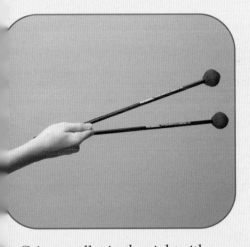

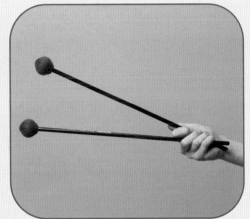

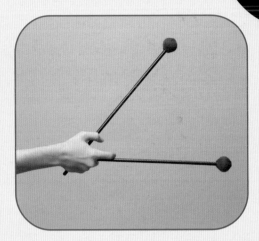

- Grip a mallet in the right either hand with the standard grip, placing the shaft between the fleshy part of the thumb and the first joint of the index finger.

- With the palm facing the floor, slide the second mallet between the index finger and middle finger so the shaft rests below the first mallet. The thumb and index finger are always between the two mallets.

- Gently close the last three fingers around the crossed mallet shafts for support with the middle finger relaxed as it curls around the shaft of the outside mallet. The thumb will rest near the top of the mallet shaft so that the tip of the thumb rests on the inside of the top mallet.

- Spread the mallets apart by sliding the thumb from the top of the mallet to the inside as the index finger presses against the inside of bottom mallet.

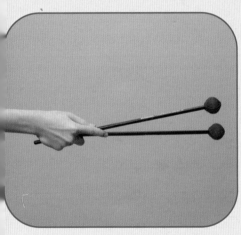

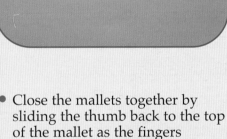

- Close the mallets together by sliding the thumb back to the top of the mallet as the fingers squeeze the mallets together.

- Point the index finger, bringing the mallets closer together, to play the smallest intervals.

- To strike with only the inner mallet, rotate the wrist on the axis of the outer mallet shaft. Use your thumb to add weight to the stroke and to help direct the mallet toward the tone bar.

- To strike with only the outer mallet, move the wrist with a motion similar to the full stroke of the snare drum. Use the index finger to direct the mallet toward the tone bar.

- The wrist naturally rotates toward the outside when holding two mallets in one hand.

- The "pinky" finger always touches the palm as it crosses over both mallet shafts at the cross point. The pinky should maintain a firm enough grip so that the mallets don't slip in the hand.

UNIT 25

Creative Tools of Music

3 = beats in a measure
2 = half note/rest receives one beat

○· = 3 beats in 3/2 time

New Notes: Concert Db, Fb;
See the position chart
in the back of this book

Key of G

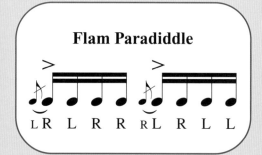

Flam Paradiddle

PORTRAIT

Igor Stravinsky

No other composer personifies Twentieth Century music more than Igor Stravinsky. Born near St. Petersburg, Russia in 1882, where his father was a singer with the Imperial Opera, Stravinsky began his musical studies at the age of nine. As a university student, he befriended the son of famous Russian composer Nicolai Rimsky-Korsakov, and soon became a private student of the composer.

After writing several successful orchestral works, Stravinsky was commissioned to write the music for the ballet *The Firebird* (1910). This brilliant score was a stunning success, and it allowed Stravinsky to break out on his own. Another famous ballet, *Petrouchka,* quickly followed, but his score for the ballet *The Rite of Spring* (1913) was the defining moment for the young composer and helped to usher in a new period of music. This ballet, with its biting dissonance, constantly changing time signatures, new orchestral colors, and savage rhythmic effects caused a near-riot at its first performance.

Throughout his long and illustrious career, Stravinsky composed numerous works for ballet, opera, orchestra, chorus, large and small ensemble, solo voice, and piano. Stravinsky died in New York in 1971, and was buried in Venice, Italy.

152 *Concert G Major Scale*

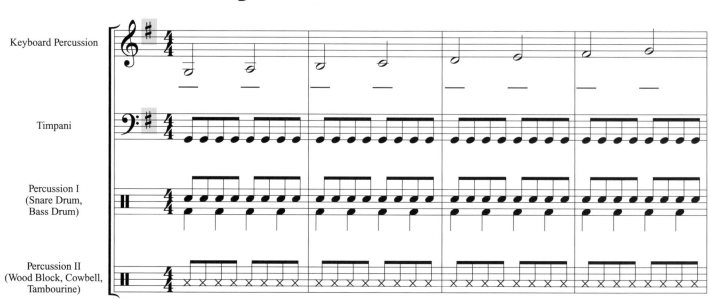

ne 152 continued

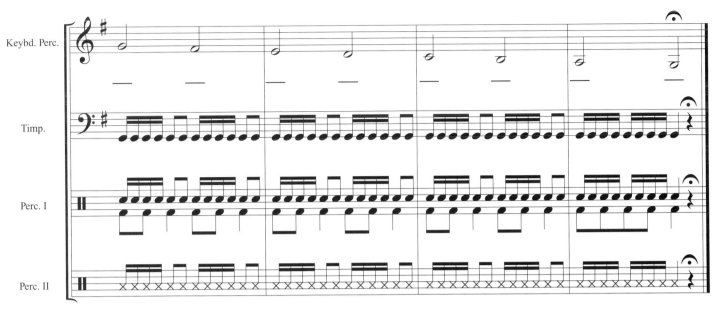

153 *Pavane*

MAURICE RAVEL, France

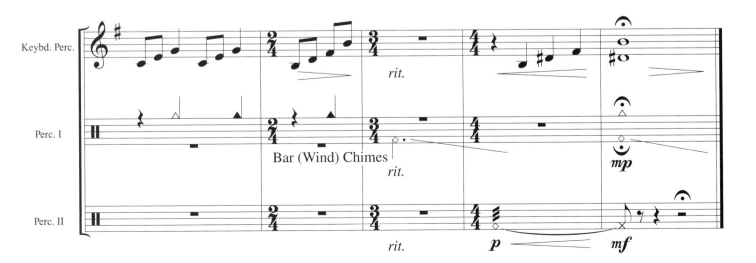

154 *Dissymetric*

155 *Bolero Nuevo*

Keyboard Percussion / Timpani / Percussion I (Snare Drum, Castanets, Bongos) / Percussion II (Tambourine)

156 Hungarian Folk Song

BÉLA BARTÓK, Hungary

157 *Danse Infernale (1910)*

IGOR STRAVINSKY, Russia, France, U.S.A.

158 Satin Doll   CD :70

Music by DUKE ELLINGTON

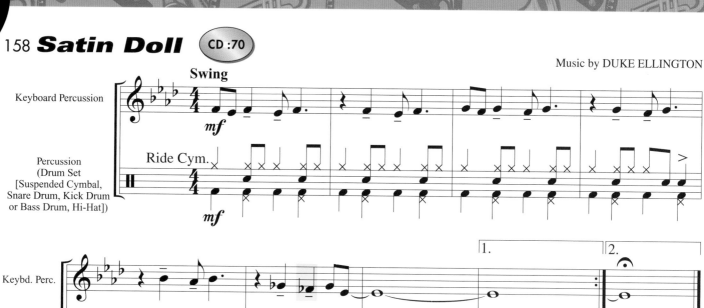

159 The Entertainer   CD :71

SCOTT JOPLIN, U.S.A.

160 **I Got Rhythm**   CD :72

Music and Lyrics by
GEORGE GERSHWIN and IRA GERSHWIN

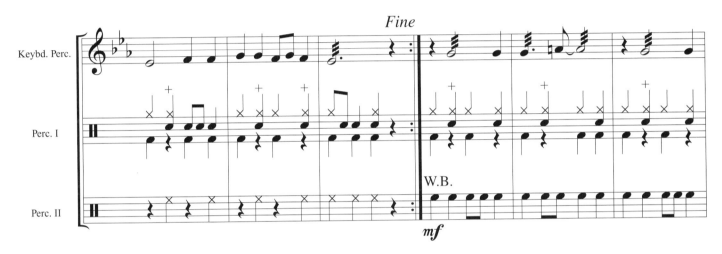

Band @ Home

LESSON 1

1. Practice singing a concert B♭ and check by playing the note on your instrument to see how accurate you were.

2. Practice "Pavane" and "Bolero Nuevo" and then perform for your family and friends.

3. Practice the Flam Paradiddle from slow to fast to slow and Accent Dexterity Exercises #1–36 at a variety of dynamic levels.

LESSON 2

1. Practice singing a concert B♭ and check by playing the note on your instrument to see how accurate you were.

2. Practice "Danse Infernale" and then perform for your family and friends.

3. Compose a piece with your own notation.

4. Practice 3-mallet technique.

LESSON 3

1. Continue composing a piece with your own notation. Choose the instruments you would like to perform it.

2. Practice Accent Dexterity Exercise #36.

3. Practice four-way coordination by air drumming.

UNIT 26 IS PRESENTED BY YOUR TEACHER

UNIT 27

161 Mouthpiece Echo Warm-Up

162 Concert F Relay

163 Building Concert F

164 Renaissance Chorale

WOLFGANG DACHSTEIN, Germany
Harmonized by JOHANN SEBASTIAN BACH, Germany

165 As Time Goes By

Words and Music by HERMAN HUPFELD

166 Taking the "Fifth"

167 More Open Fifths

168 *Semiramide*

GIOACCHINO ROSSINI, Italy

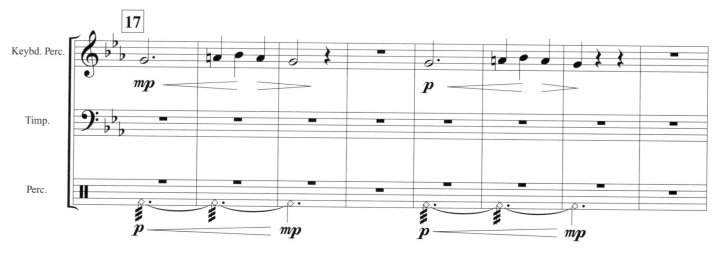

169 *Irish Melody*

Traditional, Ireland

Band @ Home

LESSON 1

1. Remember all of the fundamentals that are necessary in order for you to produce your best sound (posture, hand positions, etc.) Also, remember to warm up properly.

2. Practice "Renaissance Chorale" and "As Time Goes By."

LESSON 2

1. Perform "Partners Tuning" exercise with another student.

2. Practice "Semiramide" and "Irish Melody."

LESSON 3

1. Perform your favorite pieces from this unit for your family and friends.

2. Listen to recordings and see if you can hear all the instruments equally well.

UNIT 28

170 "Firebird" Warm-Up

IGOR STRAVINSKY, Russia, France, U.S.A.

171 Concert B♭ Scale in Thirds

172 Concert A♭ Scale in Thirds

173 Clarke Bars

174 *Three-Way Quarters*

175 *Three-Way Eighths*

line 175 continued

176 *Old Time Rock & Roll*

Words and Music by
GEORGE JACKSON and
THOMAS E. JONES III

UNIT 29

The Art of Playing Chimes

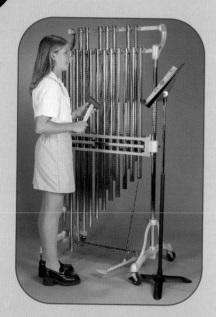

Rest Position

- Place the music stand close to the side of the chimes and use peripheral vision to see the chimes while watching the music and the conductor.

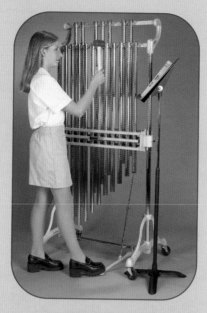

Ready Position

- Depress the pedal mechanism on the chimes to let the tubes resonate. Use a mallet or hammer specially designed for concert chimes.

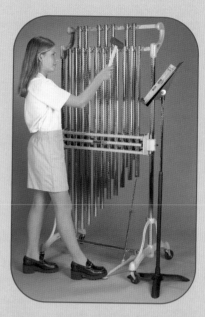

Play Position

- Make a quick stroke to strike the side of the cap on the tube.

177 *Finlandia*

JEAN SIBELIUS, Finland

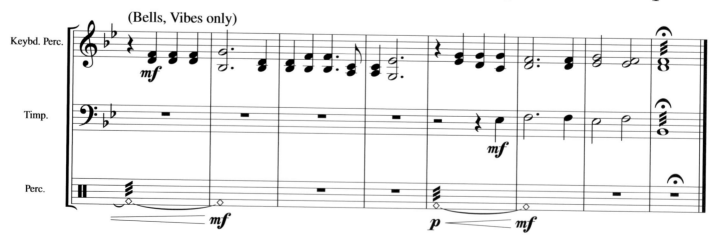

178 *Londonderry Air*

Traditional, Ireland

179 The Minstrel Boy

THOMAS MOORE, Ireland

180 Carnival of Venice

JULIUS BELLAK
Folk Song, Italy

181 Can You Read My Mind?

Lyrics by LESLIE BRICUSSE
Music by JOHN WILLIAMS

182 Shenandoah

Traditional, U.S.A.

The Art of Playing Güiro

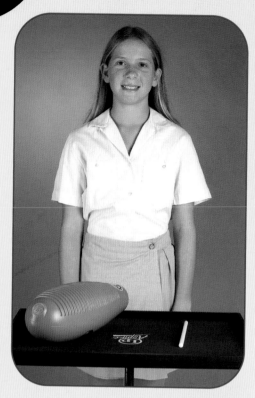

Rest Position

- The Güiro should be placed on a padded surface to make their pickup and replacement as silent as possible.

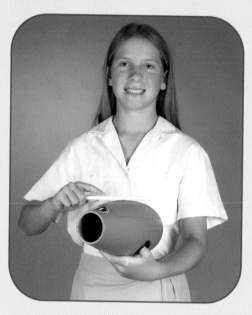

Ready Position

- Insert your thumb and middle finger into the holes cut into the bottom of the güiro. Hold the güiro at chest level, parallel to the floor.

- A tapered scraper works best to produce a variety of sounds and dynamics.

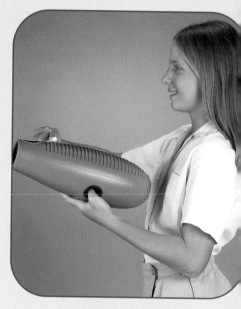

Play Position

- Draw the scraper across the grooves. Long and short scrapes can be played to match the note values indicated in the music.

- Scrape away from your body for long notes and toward your body for short notes.

- When the rhythms are fast, alternate directions on every note.

- A slow scrape produces a soft sound, while a fast scrape is generally louder.

Creative Tools of Music

Cantabile—perform in a smooth, flowing, and melodious singing style

D.S. al Coda—return to the sign and play the Coda ending

Sforzando (*sfz*)—perform with a sudden strong accent on a single note or chord

2 measure repeat—play the two previous measures over again

Rallentando (rall.)—gradually slower and slightly broader

Rubato—a flexible tempo involving slight accelerandos and rallentandos

New Notes: See the position chart in the back of this book for any unfamiliar notes

183 **The Washington Post** CD :73

JOHN PHILIP SOUSA, U.S.A.
Arranged by MICHAEL STORY (ASCAP)

Be prepared for you or your standmate to quickly turn the page.

UNIT 30—33

Line 183 continued

ne 183 continued

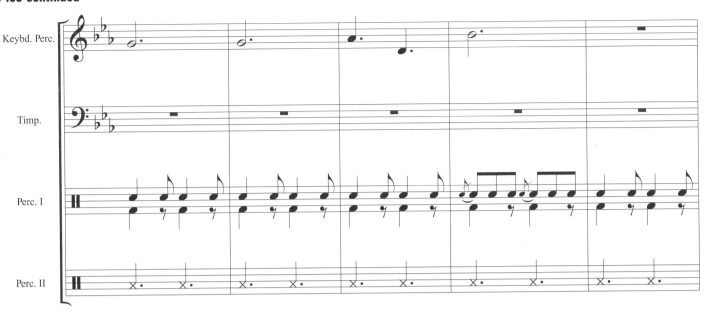

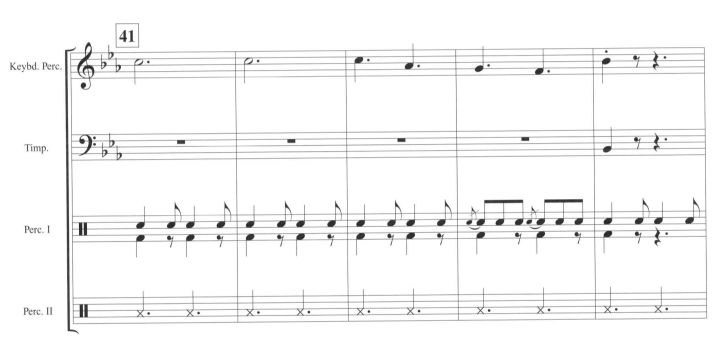

184 Emerald Peak Melody

185 Emerald Peak

CD :74

MICHAEL STORY, U.S.A.

ine 185 continued

Be prepared for you or your standmate to quickly turn the page.

Line 185 continued

line 185 continued

186 E♭ Isolation

187 **F Isolation**

188 **Song Without Words** CD :75

GUSTAV HOLST, England
Arranged by ROBERT W. SMITH

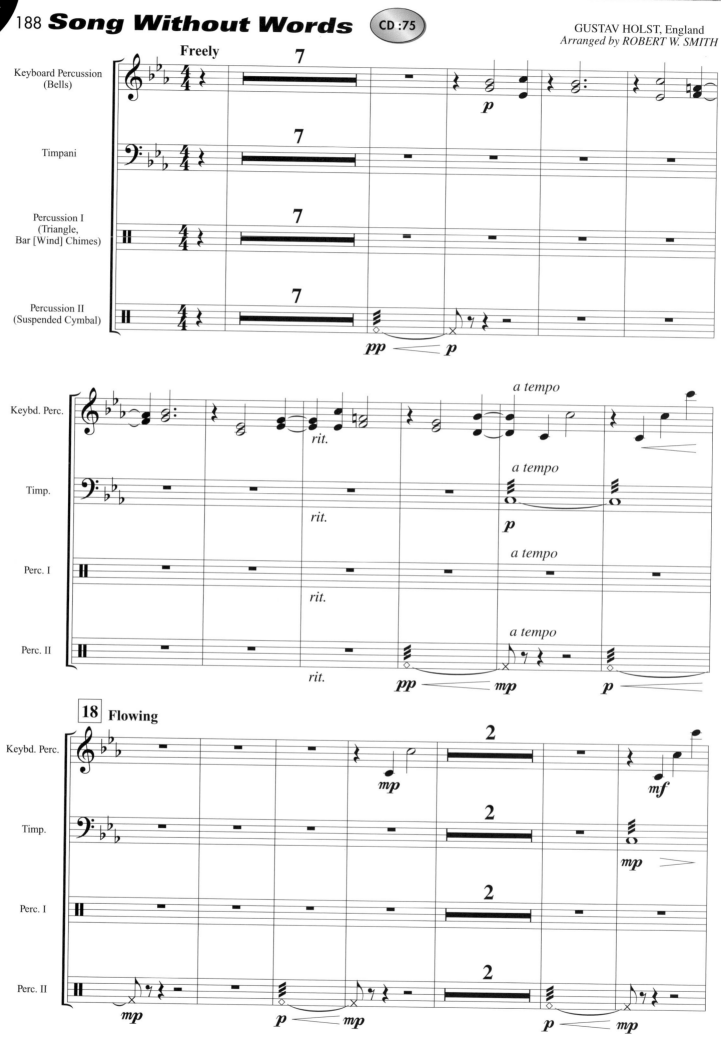

ine 188 continued

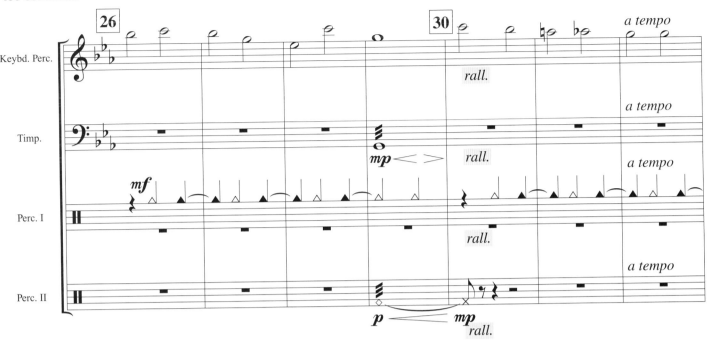

189 *Holst Melody*

GUSTAV HOLST, England

190 **Guantanamera** CD :76

Original Words and Music by JOSÉ FERNANDEZ
Music adaptation by PETE SEEGER
Lyric adaptation by HECTOR ANGULO
Arranged by ROBERT W. SMITH

ne 190 continued

Be prepared for you or your standmate to quickly turn the page.

Line 190 continued

ne 190 continued

Be prepared for you or your standmate to quickly turn the page.

Line 190 continued

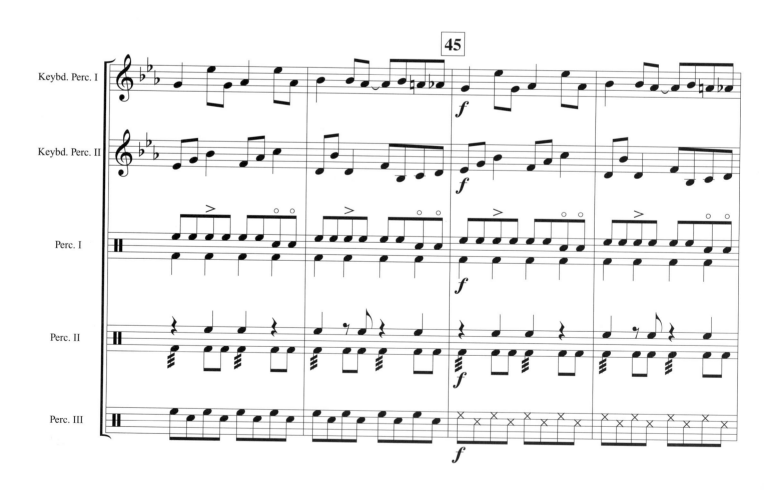

UNIT 30-33

line 190 continued

225

191 *Proud Mary* CD :77

Words and Music by JOHN FOGERTY
Arranged by MICHAEL STORY

ne 191 continued

Be prepared for you or your standmate to quickly turn the page.

Line 191 continued

Line 191 continued

192 The Rose

Words and Music by
AMANDA McBROOM

193 Contrasts

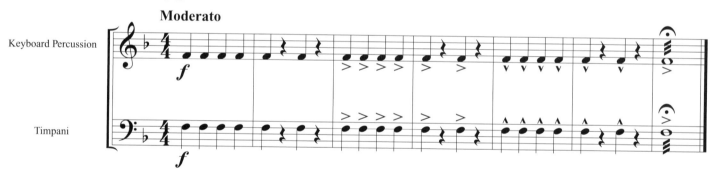

194 **Star Wars**
(Main Theme)

CD :78

By **JOHN WILLIAMS**
Arranged by MICHAEL STORY

1st and 2nd endings—play the 1st ending, repeat the section and play only the 2nd ending the second time (20)

accelerando (accel.)—gradually faster (156)

accent (>)—play the note with more emphasis (20)

accidental (♯, ♭, ♮)—a sharp, flat, or natural not indicated in the key signature (–)

allegretto—moderately quick tempo (92)

allegro—fast tempo (20)

anacrusis—one or more notes that come before the first full measure (12)

andante—moderately slow (walking) tempo (20)

arpeggio—the notes of a chord played in succession 1–3–5–8–5–3–1 (104)

articulation—a slight interruption of the air stream with the tongue (68)

a tempo—return to the previous tempo (164)

binary form (AB)—form consisting of two parts (104)

cantabile—perform in a smooth, flowing, and melodious, singing style (208)

chromatic scale—a scale made up of only half steps (68)

compound meter—meter in which each beat in a measure can be divided by three (6/8, 9/8, 12/8) (156)

crescendo, cresc. (———)—gradually get louder (68)

cut time(¢)—a symbol for the 2/2 time signature (114)

D.C. al Coda—return to the beginning and play the Coda ending (164)

D.C. al Fine—return to the beginning and play to the fine (76)

D.S. al Coda—return to the sign and play the Coda ending (208)

D.S. al Fine—return to the sign and play to the fine (44)

decrescendo, decresc. (———)—gradually get softer (68)

diminuendo, dim.—gradually softer (68)

divisi—divide into two or more parts (20, 44)

double stops—two notes played simultaneously on a keyboard percussion insturment (92)

dynamics—musical performance levels of loud and soft (12)

enharmonics—notes that are spelled differently, but sound the same (54)

fine—the end (–)

forte (f)—loud (12)

fortissimo (ff)—very loud (76)

fortepiano (fp)—play loud and then immediately play soft (164)

half step—the distance between two adjacent notes (68)

interval—the distance between two pitches (54)

key signature—flats and sharps placed immediately following the clef, indicating which notes are to be altered throughout the piece (12)

legato—play smooth and connected without interruption between the notes (12)

lento—slow (84)

maestoso—majestic or stately (122)

major—a sequence of notes that defines the tonality of the major scale (92)

major scale—a series of stepwise notes, up or down, with the ascending step pattern of whole, whole, half, whole, whole, whole, half (92)

marcato (ʌ)—a style of playing notes emphasized and slightly separated (76)

mezzo forte (mf)—medium loud (12)

mezzo piano (mp)—medium soft (12)

minor—a sequence of notes that defines the tonality of the minor scale (92)

minor scale (natural)—a series of stepwise notes, up or down, with the ascending step pattern of whole, half, whole, whole, half, whole, whole (92)

molto—very or much (178)

moderato—moderate or medium tempo (20)

ostinato—a repeated melodic or rhythmic pattern (20)

pentatonic scale—a five-note scale (68, 92)

phrase—a musical sentence or statement (12)

phrasing—the art of playing musical sentences or statements (84)

piano (p)—soft (12)

pianissimo (pp)—very soft (76)

poco a poco—little by little (68)

rallentando (rall.)—gradually slower and slightly broader (208)

repeat—a symbol that indicates to go back and play the section of music again (12)

ritardando, rit.—gradually slower (122)

rubato—a flexible tempo involving slight accelerandos and rallentandos (208)

scale—a series of tones arranged in a set pattern from low to high or high to low (12)

sforzando (sfz)—perform with a sudden strong accent on a single note or chord (208)

shape and contour—the direction of a melody through dynamics, pitch levels, and rhythm (122)

simile—play in the same style (54)

simple meter—meter in which each beat in a measure can be divided by two (2/4, 3/4, 4/4) (156)

slur—a curved line placed above or below two or more pitches indicating that they are to be performed smoothly and connected (30)

soli—a line of music played by a small group of instruments (122)

staccato—play the note lightly and detached (12)

subdivide—break down a beat into smaller divisions (156)

tenuto (▬)—a symbol that means to play the note full value (12)

ternary form (ABA)—form consisting of three sections (112)

texture—the vertical elements of music, including melodies, harmonies, rhythms, and instruments (178)

tie—a curved line connecting two notes of the same pitch, indicating that they are to be played as if they were one note (-)

time signature—a symbol placed at the beginning of the staff where the top number indicates the number of beats per measure and the bottom number what kind of note receives one beat (12)

trill (tr)—a musical symbol or term meaning to alternate rapidly between two adjacent pitches (172)

tutti—all play (122)

variation—a restatement that retains some features of the original idea or theme (30)

Quarter 1

Quarter 2

Quarter 3

Quarter 4

In 2 and in 6

The Percussive Arts Society International Drum Rudiments

I. ROLL RUDIMENTS

A. Single Stroke Roll Rudiments

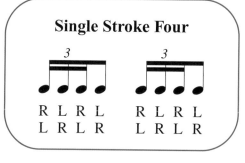

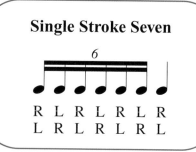

B. Multiple Bounce Roll Rudiments

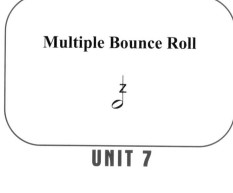

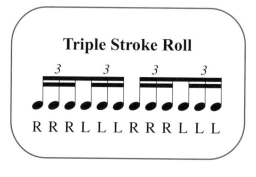

C. Double Stroke Open Roll Rudiments

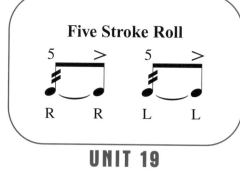

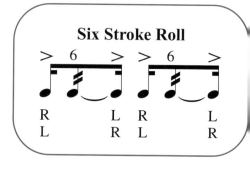

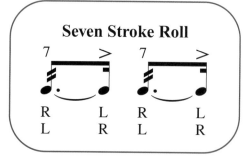

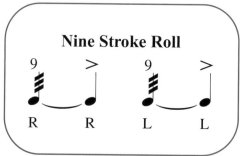

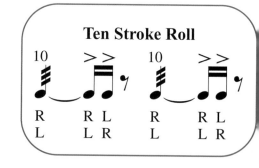

C. Double Stroke Open Roll Rudiments, continued on top of next page

C. Double Stroke Open Roll Rudiments, continued.

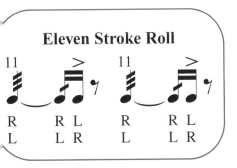

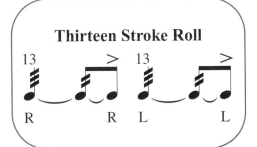

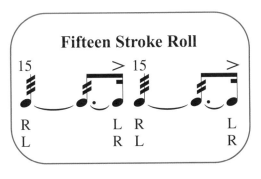

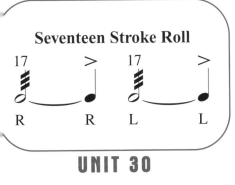

UNIT 30

II. DIDDLE RUDIMENTS

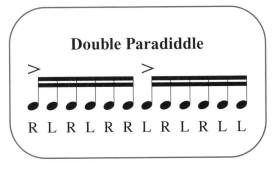

UNIT 10

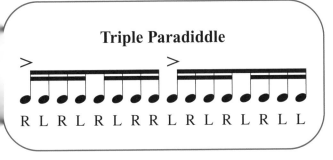

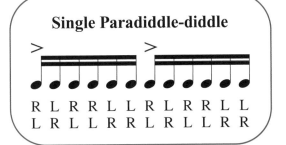

PERCUSSION RUDIMENTS

III. FLAM RUDIMENTS

Flam

L R   R L

UNIT 12

Flam Accent

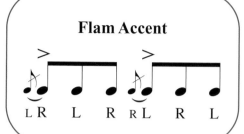

L R L R RL R L

Flam Tap

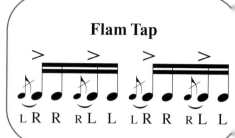

L R R RL L L R R RL L

UNIT 24

Flamacue

L R L R L L R
R L R L R R L

Flam Paradiddle

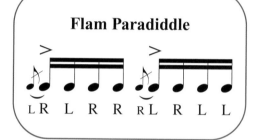

L R L R R RL R L L

Single Flammed Mill

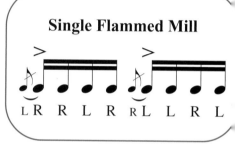

L R R L R RL L R L

Flam Paradiddle-diddle

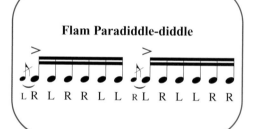

L R L R R L L RL R L L L R R

Pataflafla

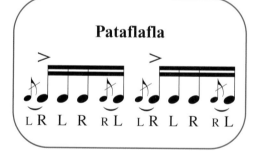

L R L R RL L R L R RL

Swiss Army Triplet

L R R L L R R L L R
R L L R R L L R

Inverted Flam Tap

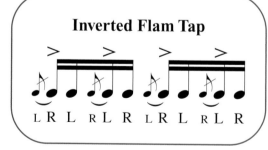

L R L R L R L R L R L R

Flam Drag

L R L L R RL R R L

236

PERCUSSION RUDIMENTS

V. DRAG RUDIMENTS

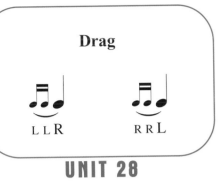

Drag

L L R   R R L

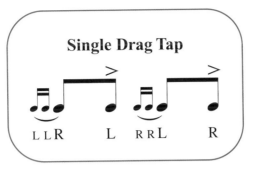

Single Drag Tap

L L R   L   R R L   R

UNIT 28

Double Drag Tap

L L R L L R L R R L R R L R

Lesson 25

L L R L R L L R L R
R R L R L R R L R L

Single Dragadiddle

R R L R R L L R L L

Drag Paradiddle

R L L R L R R L R R L R L L

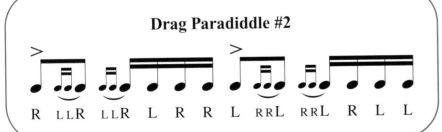

Drag Paradiddle #2

R L L R L L R L R R L R R L R R L R L L

Single Ratamacue

L L R L R L R R L R L R

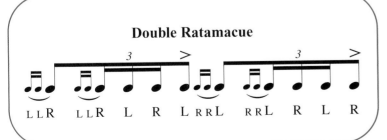

Double Ratamacue

L L R L L R L R L R R L R R L R L R

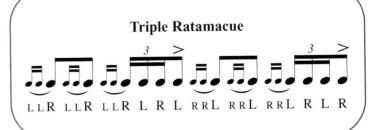

Triple Ratamacue

L L R L L R L L R L R L R R L R R L R R L R L R

Reprinted by permission of the Percussive Arts Society, Inc., 701 NW Ferris, Lawton, OK 73507-5442:
e-mail: percarts@pas.org • web: www.pas.org

Concert A

Concert A♭

Concert B♭

Concert C

Concert D

Your teacher will assign an Accent Dexterity Exercise for Drums and Auxiliary Percussion.

Concert D♭

Concert E♭

Concert F

Concert G

Concert B♭ Chromatic

Two-Octave Concert F Chromatic

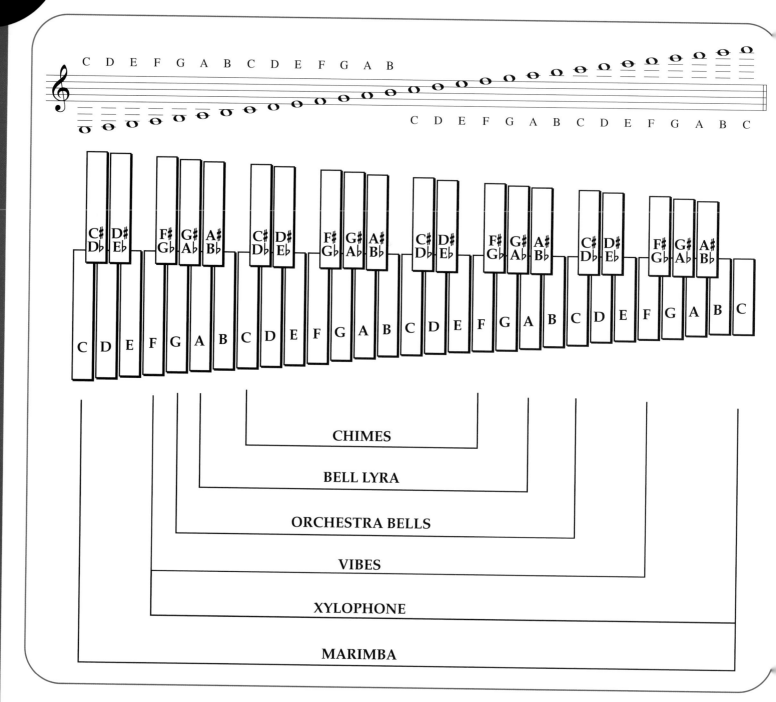

- The Orchestra Bells/Glockenspiel sounds two octaves higher than written. The standard range is 2 1/2 octaves.

- The Xylophone sounds one octave higher than written. The standard range is 3 1/2 octaves.

- The Vibraphone sounds as written. The standard range is 3 octaves.

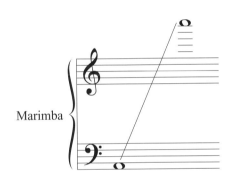

- The Marimba sounds as written. The standard range is 4 1/3 octaves.

- The Chimes sounds one octave higher than written. The standard range is 1 1/2 octaves.

Accent Dexterity Exercises

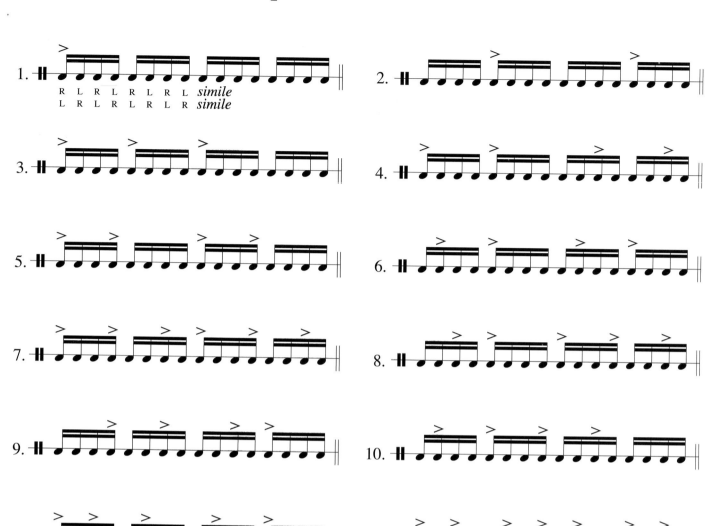

Stroke Dexterity Exercises

1.	R	R	R	R		R	R	R	R		L	L	L	L		L	L	L	L
2.	R	R	R	R		L	L	L	L		R	R	R	R		L	L	L	L
3.	R	R	R	L		R	R	R	L		R	R	R	L		R	R	R	L
4.	L	L	L	R		L	L	L	R		L	L	L	R		L	L	L	R
5.	R	L	L	L		R	L	L	L		R	L	L	L		R	L	L	L
6.	L	R	R	R		L	R	R	R		L	R	R	R		L	R	R	R
7.	R	R	L	L		R	R	L	L		R	R	L	L		R	R	L	L
8.	R	L	R	L		R	L	R	L		R	L	R	L		R	L	R	L
9.	R	L	R	L		R	R	R	R		L	R	L	R		L	L	L	L
10.	R	L	R	L		R	L	R	R		R	L	R	L		R	L	R	R
11.	L	R	L	R		L	R	L	L		L	R	L	R		L	R	L	L
12.	R	L	R	L		R	R	L	L		R	L	R	L		R	R	L	L
13.	L	R	L	R		L	L	R	R		L	R	L	R		L	L	R	R
14.	R	L	R	R		L	L	R	R		L	R	L	L		R	R	L	L
15.	R	L	R	R		L	R	L	L		R	L	R	R		L	R	L	L
16.	R	R	L	R		L	L	R	L		R	L	R	R		L	R	L	L
17.	R	L	L	R		L	R	R	L		R	L	L	R		L	R	R	L
18.	R	L	R	L		R	L	R	R		L	R	L	R		L	R	L	L
19.	R	L	R	L		R	R	L	R		L	R	L	R		L	L	R	L
20.	R	L	R	L		R	L	L	R		L	R	L	R		L	R	R	L